PENANCE
CELEBRATIONS

Canadian Conference of Catholic Bishops
Ottawa, Canada

Approved by the National Office for Liturgy
for use in Canada

Edited by:
National Liturgical Office

Published by:
Publications Service

Canadian Conference of Catholic Bishops
90 Parent Avenue
Ottawa, Ontario K1N 7B1
Canada

ISBN 0-88997-043-2

Legal deposit: National Library, Ottawa, Canada.

Printed and bound in Canada by Tri-Graphic Printing (Ottawa) Limited.

TABLE OF CONTENTS

The Lord, at the beginning of his preaching, invited his followers to repentance: turn from sin and believe the Gospel (see Mark 1: 15). Jesus gave his life to enable all to live the life of grace and turn away from sin. His desire for sinners was that they be reconciled with the Father. In his teaching Jesus asks us to be children of light and not darkness. His way to realize this was through forgiveness, mercy and compassion. This is shown in his welcoming approach to sinners.

Death to sin and resurrection to new life is the paschal mystery. It is this mystery, now lived by the followers of Jesus, that makes possible reconciliation within the Christian community.

After his resurrection, to continue the ministry of forgiveness, Jesus sent the Holy Spirit upon the apostles. The responsibility of the apostles was to continue the preaching of repentance; calling people from sin and to life in God. The Church today continues this ministry of reconciliation (see *Redemptor Hominis,* no. 20). To make this possible the new *Rite of Penance* was issued on December 2, 1973. In this revised rite the celebration of the sacrament is placed within the context of the word of God. Penance celebrations are strongly encouraged as excellent ways for the Christian community to experience conversion from sin and life for God (see *Rite of Penance,* nos. 36, 37).

At the request of the Episcopal Commission for Liturgy, the National Liturgical Office has prepared this book of *Penance Celebrations.* It presents insights to help see the place of penance celebrations in parish and community life; assistance for the planning of these celebrations; and model outlines for these celebrations, as well as for the examination of conscience.

It is our prayer that this book will assist the parish community to continue its efforts to hear the Lord's call to conversion and in turn will be at peace with God and one another.

Sincerely in the Lord,

Bishop of Peterborough
Acting Chairman
Episcopal Commission for Liturgy

INTRODUCTION

What is a penance celebration?

A bible service: When God's people gather to listen to God's word, to reflect on it, and to respond in praise, prayer, and action, they are celebrating a service of the word or a bible service. This is true when two or three gather in Jesus' name (see Mt. 18: 19-20), and when many people come together in church for a solemn celebration. In every bible service, God calls us to repentance and renewal through the saving power of his word.

A penance celebration is a form of bible service, but one which is more directly concerned with our conversion and renewal. As the readings are proclaimed and preached upon, the Spirit stirs up our hearts, and invites us to be converted, turning away from our sins and turning back to our forgiving Father. We are assured of forgiveness and are invited to renew our lives through the saving death and rising of our Lord Jesus Christ.

Relationship with the sacrament of penance: A penance celebration may be related to the celebration of the sacrament of reconciliation in one of several ways:

• *Directly:* The penance service may be the liturgy of the word celebrated during the second or third rites of penance:

□ The second rite is the reconciliation of a number of persons during the penance celebration, with individual confession and individual absolution (see *Rite of Penance,*[1] nos. 22-30, 48-59). Except in small groups or in a retreat setting, however, this form of celebration can become lengthy and unsatisfactory.

□ The third rite is the reconciliation of a number of persons with a general confession and general absolution (see *Rite,* nos. 31-35, 60-66).

• *Indirectly:* The penance celebration may lead to reconciliation in the sacrament of penance immediately after the service or at a later date, or it may simply help

---

[1] *Rite of Penance* (1975, CCC, 90 Parent Avenue, Ottawa, Ontario K1N 7B1).

5

a person to deepen his or her spirit of repentance and love (see *Rite,* no. 4); in due time, the person will be ready for the sacrament of reconciliation.

This is the form most familiar in North American parishes, and for this reason the celebration outlines in this book follow such an approach.

Since the sacrament of reconciliation is not directly involved in this celebration, any believing Christian — Catholic or a member of another Church, living in sin or in grace, in touch with the Church or distant from it, ready to return to the Lord or ready to take only a first step toward him — may take part with spiritual profit. Penance celebrations can provide an opening to the grace of conversion for those who want to return but who are hesitant, bewildered, or confused about the way to follow. In a penance celebration, the Holy Spirit may touch the hearts of all who are of good will, or who want to come closer to God.

*   *   *

Penance celebration: We are celebrating because God has saved us from the power of sin and the kingdom of Satan, and has brought us into the kingdom of light. Our loving Father has saved us and reconciled us to himself, and made us his beloved children through the obedient death of his Son on the cross, and through his glorious resurrection.

BIBLE

The bible is important in the life of the Church. Though most of us grew up in an age when we neglected the direct reading of God's word, the Vatican Council has called us back to our tradition of a "warm and living love" for the scriptures (Liturgy constitution, no. 24). In the bible God reveals his forgiving love in Christ, and the Spirit makes these words live in those who hear with faith.

In its document on revelation, the Council speaks of revelation in tradition and scripture, and describes the firm place of the scriptures in the life and prayer of the Christian community. The relationship of scripture and liturgy is mentioned often in the Liturgy constitution (see especially nos. 24, 51, 109, 121). Biblical imagery has strongly influenced the Vatican II documents, and will continue to direct the present and future life of the Church (see Church constitution, no. 6; Liturgy constitution, no. 6).

The public proclamation of the scriptures is part of each liturgical celebration now. For this to be truly fruitful, however, congregation, readers, religious and clergy need to be people of the book. Daily reading from the scriptures forms the basis for our prayer and Christian living. If we open our hearts to hear the Spirit and to follow his guidance, we can be more confident that we are following Christ.

Celebrations during the liturgical year

During the past decade or so, we have become used to the idea of having a penance celebration during Lent and Advent each year. There are many other times when a form of penance celebration may be profitable for the growth of grace and love in the community.

The strong seasons are the times surrounding the major feasts of Easter and Christmas. These seasons of the liturgical year are the weeks which prepare for, celebrate, and meditate on the death-resurrection and the incarnation of the Lord.

Lent-Easter

Lent: This is the major penitential season of the liturgical year. Many opportunities are present to have penitential celebrations during this season:

• *At the beginning* of the season, within the first few days after Ash Wednesday, or during the first full week in Lent, a penance celebration provides an opportunity for all Christians to begin to turn back to Christ.

• *Throughout the lenten season,* our Lord continues to call us to believe in the Good News of our salvation, to repent of our sins, and to turn back to God (see Mk. 1: 15). Conversion is the goal for Lent.

• *Special celebrations:* Besides parish penance celebrations during Lent, special celebrations may be held for the aged, the sick, school communities, organizations, and committees. Individual families or groups of families may wish to have their own celebration during this time.

Close to Easter: Lent ends before the Holy Thursday evening celebration of the Lord's supper, when the Easter triduum begins. It is desirable to encourage the entire parish community to celebrate the sacrament of reconciliation before the end of Lent. In this way, all will be ready to share fully in the paschal celebration of the suffering, death and rising of the Lord Jesus, and to celebrate our share in his paschal mystery.

Pope John XXIII suggested that Catholics should seek to be reconciled before Holy Week, so that they would be ready to take part fully in all the celebrations of the week. More and more parishes are encouraging their members to celebrate penance celebrations early, before Holy Week begins. Now they avoid the last-minute line-ups, and are able to experience the Easter triduum as days reserved for public worship, personal prayer, and deep reflection.

Easter season: This season is seven weeks long, begins with the Easter vigil, and continues until Pentecost. It is a continuation and completion of the work of conversion accomplished during Lent. The Lord is the good shepherd and the one who brings the peace of the gospel to those who turn their hearts to him. He is the vine and we are his branches. Penance celebrations held during this season will enable the parish and groups to experience the mercy, compassion, and peace which are great Easter gifts of the Lord. It is a blessed time for many to live the new Easter life with greater intensity, wisdom, and justice.

Advent-Christmas

The Christmas cycle includes a period of *preparation* (Advent), *celebration* (Christmas octave), and the *continuation* of the celebration (Epiphany and Baptism of the Lord). The central purpose of this period of about seven weeks is to celebrate the incarnation: God loves us so much that he sent his Son to become one of us and to save us by his dying and rising (see Jn. 3: 16-17).

Advent: Penance celebrations held during the Advent season provide us with the opportunity to hear again the cry of John the Baptist: "Make straight the way of the Lord" (see Mk. 1: 3). As individuals and communities, we are being called to believe the gospel and repent. The Advent penance celebration is an excellent opportunity for the community to examine its collective conscience on how it is working to build up the kingdom. Individuals are to look into their lives and see whether prayer and action, love and mercy are as good as Jesus wants them to be.

There are two distinct but related stages in Advent. The first stage begins with the First Sunday of Advent and lasts up to December 16. It continues the spirit of the final weeks of ordinary times by reflecting on the end of time and the coming of the Lord's kingdom in final glory. On December 17 our attention turns to our preparation for Christmas as the celebration of the incarnation. Like the paschal mystery, the incarnation looks at several events as one mystery of God's love: by the power of the Holy Spirit, the Son of God becomes one of us in the womb of Mary; Jesus is born at Bethlehem; and the other mysteries of the childhood of Christ are remembered.

Penance celebrations held during the time of Advent for the parish community, the sick, the school community, organizations, and committees should be planned to take advantage of the riches present in this season.

Christmas: The heart of this season is the Christmas octave, lasting from Christmas eve to New Year's day. The celebration continues until the feast of the Baptism of the Lord. The Church celebrates the incarnation of God's Son as one of us. We praise the Father who loves us so much that he sent his Son to be one of us (see Jn. 3: 16). We praise God whose eternal Son is now our brother. Christmas is a memorial in which we recall the incarnation and birth of Jesus. The eternal Word brings new light into the world and restores the gift of eternal life to us.

During the octave we celebrate because the Son of God has become one of us, and was born to be our savior. The savior is the Son of God and the light of the world. He cleanses us in baptism and renews us by pouring his Spirit into our hearts.

A parish may encourage family penance celebrations at this time of the year which highlights the major dimensions of the Lord's coming to gift his people with life and light.

Continuation of the season:

• *Epiphany:* This feast celebrates the incarnation and work of the Son of God among us. On the Epiphany we celebrate the revelation that God makes to the world in Jesus Christ. He is the image of the God we cannot see. He is the light of the world (see Jn. 1: 4-5) and leads us back to the Father.

• *Baptism of the Lord:* At the beginning of his public life Jesus was baptized by John in the Jordan. The Father proclaimed that Jesus was the beloved Son; the Spirit was poured upon him to send him on his mission of freeing us from sin and of healing the world. The Church sees our Lord's baptism as a model of our own. In the blessing of baptismal water at the Easter vigil, his baptism is referred to as one of the signs of God's power at work among us.

The feast of the Baptism of the Lord completes the work of the Christmas season. We have recalled God's marvellous deeds in the incarnation and birth of the savior. His call to conversion is answered and we are committed to work with him for the glory of God and the salvation of all his people.

Penance celebrations highlighting the themes of these feasts help the community to respond in faith to be the light of nations and the source of life for the world. In preparation for baptism, recommended for the feast of the Baptism of the Lord, the parish may gather parents and friends of those to be baptized to celebrate anew the mercy and forgiveness brought to the world through the Lord's baptism.

Ordinary Time

In comparison with the Easter and Christmas cycles, ordinary time is set in a "low key." Lasting 33 or 34 weeks, ordinary time covers almost two-thirds of the Church's year of grace. It comes in two periods, after the Baptism of the Lord to Ash Wednesday, and after Pentecost to the beginning of Advent. It provides us with a quiet time to reflect on the meaning of God's gift to us in Christ, our attitude toward creation, our prayer life, and our service to others — in other words, our life as Church.

Between the Christmas and Easter cycles: After the feast of the Lord's Baptism in January ordinary time begins. It continues the Epiphany theme of the Lord's mission and reveals God's presence and action through Christ and his Church. In some Churches, this period is known as the time after Epiphany, and is seen as a continuation of the Lord's manifestation among his people. This season continues until Lent begins.

Between the Easter and Christmas cycles: Following the Pentecost celebration ordinary time resumes for some six months. The example and teaching of Jesus and his apostles and prophets are presented to us each week to guide us. During the final weeks, especially in November, ordinary time looks ahead to the end of time and the coming of Christ as our judge — leading easily into the celebration of Advent.

Penance celebrations: The quiet nature of ordinary time provides many occasions for penance celebrations. In developing these celebrations, the opening of the rich treasures of the word of God can be realized. Important gospel readings touching the heart of penance and the call for conversion may be used on different occasions for penance celebrations.

Readings may be selected to correspond with the spirit of the liturgical year. For example, in selecting a reading for year B, one would look first at the gospel of Mark. When an Old Testament reading is selected it is chosen in relationship to the gospel.

The *Rite of Penance,* nos. 176-201, lists 26 gospel readings for penance celebrations: 11 from Matthew, 1 from Mark, 8 from Luke, and 6 from John. In planning penance celebrations these suggested readings provide a sound relationship with the flow of the liturgical celebration of ordinary time.

Mary and the Saints

The Church honors Mary and the saints because Christ has first honored them. He has chosen them, filled them with his Spirit of grace, and called them to serve him in a particular way. Their lives are models for us in their faith, their obedience, their love, their total self-giving to Christ and his people. We do not imitate them in the particular events of their lives as much as in their devotion to God and to his will for them.

The saints are signs of Christ's victory over sin (Liturgy constitution, nos. 103, 104). As his paschal mystery took possession of their lives, so it can and will in ours. As they have been given the reward of eternal joy for their faithfulness, so too will we, if we remain faithful to the end with the grace of the Lord Jesus, who died and rose to save us all.

May we learn to love as they loved,
and to practise what they taught.[1]

In acquiring holiness in life the saints acquired a true penitential spirit. The story of the journey to sainthood of these heroes in faith gives courage and inspiration to us who live today. Penance celebrations for specific groups who honor a particular saint as their patron (e.g., Luke for physicians, Joseph for workers) may be planned.

In the planning and celebration of these services of prayer and reflection on the life of faith, a particular saint may be suggested as a model. The community may be invited to consider how this saint and other saints overcame sin by following the way of Christ; their struggle with temptation; the practice of the virtue of penance in their daily lives; and Christ as the light and source of all happiness.

---

[1] Inscription in St. Mary's Cathedral, San Francisco.

In preparation for the sacraments

Penance celebrations during the time of preparing for each sacrament are opportunities for grace and closer union in faith with others and with God. They provide opportunities for prayerful reflection on the presence of Christ among us and an openness to experience his forgiveness and mercy. The pastoral care expressed by parish leadership in arranging penance celebrations on these occasions will help those who continue to lead the life of grace to deepen this life; it will assist those who struggle with temptation and sin to hear once again the invitation of Christ, "Come follow me."

Sacraments of Christian Initiation

Baptism of adults: Lent is a time of penance and renewal (Liturgy constitution, nos. 109-110). It is the period of intense preparation for the catechumens as they prepare for baptism at the Easter vigil. For the unbaptized catechumens penance celebrations have great benefits. By taking part in these celebrations the candidates are strengthened with grace to respond to God's love for them, and are encouraged to move from sin to Christian living. During the penance celebrations they listen to the readings, sing, and pray with the community.

• The candidates who are baptized and are preparing for full communion with the believing community at the time of vigil prepare by participating in penance celebrations and the sacrament of reconciliation. The examination of conscience held during penance celebrations is also of help to the penitents as they prepare to celebrate the sacrament before Easter.

The parish is encouraged to invite the candidates to celebrate the sacrament of reconciliation just before Easter. It is recognized that Holy Thursday is the traditional day for the reconciliation of penitents in the Roman rite. In some parishes it may be better to have a celebration for the candidates on Good Friday or Holy Saturday during the day.

Children: Parents and godparents in their preparation for the baptism of a child are called to renew their own baptismal commitment to Christ (see *Baptism of Children*, Introduction, no. 5). They are invited to renew their faith in Christ and turn to a more intense way of living their covenant with God. It is the faith of believing parents and the community that the child enters through baptism. This faith at the time of baptism needs to be stirred up and made active (see 2 Tim. 1: 6). In turn the child will have the true family environment to grow in faith and love.

In light of this it becomes essential for the child's parents to examine their own way of life as a response to God's gift of spiritual life in baptism.

There may be situations in which parents are negligent in the practice of faith. In these situations there is a greater need for parents to hear God's call for conversion. This call once heard gives to the hearer the occasion to return to full worship and the sacramental life of the people of God.

The parish in its care for the faith life of parents may arrange a penance celebration in which the call for conversion is heard and celebrated. The celebration may highlight Christ as life and death; we are God's children with Christ; death to sin and rising to new life realized in Christ; the way to true happiness is living a beatitude life — the grand design for Christian living.

Confirmation:

• *Adults:* The *Rite of Christian Initiation of Adults* states that adults being initiated or welcomed into full communion are to be confirmed at the same celebration in which they are baptized or welcomed. This rite gives as normative practice the baptism, confirmation, and full participation in the eucharist during the Easter vigil. The suggestions on page 11 on penance celebrations before baptism apply equally to confirmation.

• *The young:* By their example and prayer the members of the believing community help the younger members to mature in Christian faith. In baptism we die with Christ to sin and rise to new life; we receive the Spirit of adoption and become the sons and daughters of God. In confirmation we become more perfect images of the Lord Jesus and are filled with his Holy Spirit. Thus strengthened we commit ourselves to the work of the Church and renew our covenant with God as we celebrate the eucharist.

Parish leadership should provide a penance celebration for parents, sponsors, and the candidates prior to the time of confirmation. These celebrations may focus the call of our Lord to use our gifts and talents in service to others; show how the fruits of the Spirit may be lived each day; or bring forth how the life of the Spirit is alive in this community of faith.

Eucharist: In the eucharist we are called to hear God's word in faith; to praise and thank him for his wonders among us; to eat the bread of life and drink the cup of salvation in memory of Jesus; and to go forth, renewed and strengthened, to praise God and to work for the salvation of the world.

• *First eucharist:* The parish gives praise and thanks to God in a special way when children receive communion for the first time. A penance celebration may be planned before this event. Children already introduced to such celebrations may be invited along with family and friends to hear anew the forgiving word of God filled with mercy and compassion. The celebration strengthened with music and creative responses will help unfold the truth — Christ is our savior. This celebration may focus on Christ as the one who brings us around the banquet table of life. He is the one who invites us to be guests at his table. Jesus unites us as the one family of God's children: we are called to love and care for others, and to be concerned for them. Our Lord shows the true and humble way of life to those who are his friends and co-workers.

• *Solemn annual exposition:* See pages 15-16.

Other Sacraments

Reconciliation: Through its long history, the Church has remained faithful to the example and command of Jesus to proclaim the free forgiveness of sins. This has been done in a variety of ways over the centuries. Reconciliation — making peace with God and others through the community of faith — remains the constant responsibility of the Church. Reconciliation with God and the Church is celebrated and renewed whenever the community assembles for the Lord's supper, especially every Sunday. The penitential moments within the Mass help the community members to recall their need for ongoing conversion and forgiveness.

In the sacrament of penance, the Lord is present to invite sinners to renew their baptismal commitment to live a life for God and others. The sacrament also leads the faithful to a renewed awareness of the healing power of the risen Lord.

The sacrament of penance is celebrated in three rites:

- □ Rite of reconciliation of individual penitents;
- □ Rite for reconciliation of several penitents with individual confession and absolution;
- □ Rite for reconciliation of several penitents with general confession and absolution.

● *First penance:* The child's experience of penance begins at a very young age. Penance celebrations in which the forgiving grace of Christ is opened to the child's life are outlined in the Canadian catechetical program. These celebrations may be done in groups either in a parish or school setting. Family celebrations of penance are also suggested as a means of celebrating the mercy and forgiveness of the Father's love. The Spirit opens the heart of the young to the mercy and forgiveness of the Father present in the life of Jesus. Gradually, through these celebrations and the practice of penance in daily life, children hear the call to come to the sacrament of reconciliation.

Penance celebrations presented in the Canadian catechetical program respect the growth of the child in penance. In these celebrations the word of God summons the young to conversion and a life of forgiving love lived in relationship with others. These celebrations are recommended and may be celebrated under the leadership of the priest or catechist.

Marriage: The union of a baptized man and woman in Christian marriage is a sign of God's union with his people. Marriage is also a sign of Christ's continuing love for his bride, the Church (Eph. 5: 21-23): this love is lifelong, fruitful, and totally faithful.

When two baptized persons celebrate their marriage in a spirit of faith, it is a sacrament. Normally this celebration takes place in the presence of the community of believers. Christian marriage builds the community, and is in turn supported by it.

As part of their marriage preparation, engaged couples should be given an opportunity to take part in a penance celebration. They may invite family and friends to join them for this celebration. An opportunity for individual reconciliation may also be given at the time of this celebration. A parish may hold a number of these celebrations throughout the year. These may be arranged prior to the season in which more marriages are celebrated. The community aspect of marriage may be stressed during these celebrations.

Retreats for engaged couples or engaged encounter weekends are rich occasions for the holding of penance celebrations. During these times God calls his people to a deeper life of grace, mercy, and compassion.

These celebrations may focus on the theme of new beginning; the new road of love to follow; Christ is present as at Cana; a life of service to others.

Ministries and orders: Through the Holy Spirit, God distributes many gifts and ministries in order to build up the body of Christ, the Church. Services which recognize these gifts are celebrated in praise of God's goodness, and ask his blessing on the people of God and those who serve them.

When a person is called to a particular form of service to the Christian community, the local Church announces and celebrates that call with special liturgical rites: these are called *institution to ministries* in the case of lay persons, and *ordination* when ministers are made bishops, priests, or deacons by the laying on of hands.

Preceding the actual institution to ministries or ordination, a penance celebration may be arranged for parishioners, family members, and friends who will take part in these celebrations. Scripture readings, psalms, and music may be selected to highlight the gift of faith given in baptism; fidelity to prayer in its personal and communal dimensions; service in the spirit of Matthew 25; conversion from sin to the life of grace; light overcomes darkness.

Communal anointing of the sick: The Christian Church uses many rites and blessings to show its pastoral concern for the sick; among these is the sacrament of anointing. In this sacrament of faith, Christ continues to show his love for the sick, bringing them strength to overcome temptation and anxiety. The Spirit gives grace to restore the whole person to health, to lead to a deeper trust in God, and to help the sick person to accept trials as a sharing in the death and rising of Jesus. Persons who are dangerously ill from sickness, or who are aged and in weak condition, should be anointed. The Church wants us to receive Christ's help while we are completely conscious and able to benefit more fully from his grace.

The Church continues its ministry and compassion to the sick by providing opportunities for the sick and shut-ins to participate in penance celebrations. These celebrations may take place in the church, at home, or in the hospital. Through hearing the word of God, responding to it in faith, and examining their conscience, the sick and shut-in experience anew in their lives the forgiveness and peace of Christ. The cross as symbol of salvation; the Lord as light overcoming darkness; trust in Jesus and the living of the new commandment: these may be considered as themes for these celebrations.

Other occasions for celebrations

The parish: In its story of faith, the parish has many opportunities to give praise and thanks to God for his many blessings. The parish is on its spiritual journey toward the true homeland. In this journey many high events of faith are celebrated which recognize God as the author of life.

Funerals

Christ died for us. The Father raised him to eternal life, and made him Lord of all creation. All who are baptized into his death will one day rise with him. Accordingly, the Church calls the faithful to celebrate solemnly the passage of a brother or sister to eternal life by recalling the mystery by which our Lord went that way before us, the mystery to which we now have access in the eucharist. By our celebration, we affirm our own hope in eternal life, bring consolation to the bereaved, and pray for the dead so that they may enjoy happiness with God.

A vigil or wake service may be held some time before the funeral. The service takes the form of the liturgy of the word with scripture readings, responsorial psalms, and hymns.

On occasion this service may take on a penitential quality. It may highlight the journey of faith with Christ; Christ saves us from sin and grants everlasting peace in the heavenly kingdom; all are called to live out the corporal and spiritual works of mercy.

At the time of the vigil or wake service an opportunity may be provided for individual reconciliation.

Solemn Annual Exposition

This period of time set aside by the parish focuses devotion to Christ present in the sacrament. This presence is derived from the eucharistic sacrifice and is directed to sacramental and spiritual communion. It is based on a piety which moves people to acknowledge the marvelous presence of Christ in the eucharist and calls people to a deeper participation in the Easter mystery through eucharistic adoration.

The spiritual union with Christ makes possible a close familiarity with him; gives an opportunity to pray for peace and the salvation of the world; increases faith, hope, and love, and enables the proper dispositions to emerge so that we may celebrate the memorial of the Lord with deeper devotion. In turn the covenant relationship is maintained and the whole of life is lived with strength received by sharing in the death and resurrection of Jesus. As a result, concern with good deeds done in justice and charity brings the Christian spirit alive in the midst of today's world.

The strong liturgical seasons of Advent-Christmas and Lent-Easter do not lend themselves to times of solemn annual exposition. It is recommended that this yearly celebration be held during ordinary time: following the feast of the Baptism of the Lord to Ash Wednesday; or after Pentecost to the Saturday before Advent. The time preceding the celebration of the feast of the Solemnity of the Body and Blood of the Lord, in the last part of May or early June, as well as the first three months of the school year (September-November), are suggested times for this eucharistic devotion.

Penance celebrations held before the solemn annual exposition help parishioners prepare for this special devotion of parish life. The elderly, the sick and shut-ins, parents of young children, single-parent families, parish organizations and committees may be invited to take part in these penance celebrations. Penance celebrations may center on sharing in the cross; the Good Shepherd; the Lord of all ages; Christ the source of peace and light.

Special Anniversaries

Founding and dedication: The anniversary of the founding and dedication of the parish is a rich time to acknowledge God for his sustaining power and presence. Recognition is given to those whose initial faith made possible the beginnings of this people as a parish. The present members of the parish are challenged anew to continue the journey of life and love. Gathering together to hear the word of God at the time of anniversaries affords the opportunity to celebrate anew the Good News for all who now live the Christian faith.

The parish leadership may well plan a penance celebration in which the mercy and compassion of the loving Father is made real for all who gather to give praise and thanks for the wonders of God among us.

Patron saint: Each parish lives under the saintly protection of past heroes and heroines of faith. To belong to a specific parish named in memory of the saints enables parishioners to recall the qualities of holiness lived by its patron. In celebrating the feast of its patron saint, the parish recalls his or her efforts to die to sin and to live for the Lord. The celebration calls on the people to live for the Lord with renewed vigor and courage.

Our Lord's way of life inspired the parish patron to live forth the life of faith both in word and deed. In this context, the parish may plan a penance celebration to open once more the treasures of mercy and forgiveness made possible for us through the Lord's death-resurrection.

Popular festivals: Ethnic and cultural practices are varied and rich throughout Canada. Festivals of faith marking special events are frequently celebrated by people with differing geographic backgrounds and origins. These are part of the mosaic of lived faith kept alive through authentic praise and thanks to God who first gave new life in his Son Jesus through baptism. Celebrations rooted in the paschal mystery give new hope and life to those who journey and are part of the rising generation of faith.

The oneness and peace that flow from penance celebrations during these festivals are special gifts ensuring growth in faith, hope, and love. These celebrations may recall how Christian faith developed in various cultures; the power of forgiveness in building bridges of oneness and peace among these cultures; and Christ as the way to unity while respecting diversity within God's family.

Parish organizations and groups: In living out its life the parish organizes its mission in many ways. The parish council, the CWL, and the Scout movement are examples of these expressions of the life of the parish. Parish groups bring their gifts and talents to the building up of the kingdom in the here-and-now situation. Annual celebrations by these groups are occasions to rejoice and give praise to God for his many blessings.

As these groups mark special anniversaries, celebrations of penance may be planned. These celebrations may accent that Christ is the source of new life; the Spirit calls all to peace and oneness with family, the parish, and the world; service to others is Christ's way of life.

Diocesan Feasts

Dedication: The anniversary of the dedication of the cathedral church illustrates the truth that a diocese is the temple of the living people called to give glory and thanksgiving to God. The Father is the one who in Christ calls the local Church to holiness. Under the guidance of the chief shepherd and servant, the bishop, the diocese celebrates its paschal life by marking in liturgical symbol the anniversary of dedication of the cathedral church. Conscious of its beginnings as a holy people and in tune with the efforts of many to construct a living edifice of thanks and praise, the diocese calls its members to be in touch with its roots. Christ is the center, the architect of a people who are continually called to conversion from sin and to new life in Christ. The path of Christ the leader is the one followed by those who journey to the true homeland. Christ is the way, the truth, and the life.

On this occasion the diocese may encourage a penance celebration which focuses on Christ as the cornerstone and ourselves as his living stones; he is the vine, we are his branches; all are called to witness to justice and charity; the diocese is a people of prayer and celebration.

Patron: The anniversary of the chief patron saint of the diocese provides the occasion to celebrate once more the presence of Christ in our midst. The diocesan patron is seen as one who united with Christ was obedient to the Father's will. By recalling the patron's faithfulness to the Lord's way of life on this earth, the diocesan community is assured of the promise of everlasting union with God.

A penance celebration calling us to remember we are brothers and sisters in the Lord may be held throughout the diocese on this occasion. The loving and merciful Father makes possible the oneness and unity of all. Christ the joy and hope of all the saints is the great joy and hope of all in this age.

School Community

Beginning of school year: It is recommended that the school community hold a penance celebration at the beginning of the school year. The gift of forgiveness given by the Lord and present in the lives of those who respond in faith hastens the journey to oneness of purpose and unity in life.

Major feasts: These provide rich occasions to celebrate the wonders of God. These are excellent times to experience the loving mercy of the Father. Related to the celebration of the liturgical year, these high points of grace are uplifted when the living word of God becomes present in scripture, song, and creative expression.

Closing of the year: Having lived a year of new life the school community may gather to celebrate its conversion from sin to grace. Christ shows the way to live in harmony and challenges the use of gifts and talents in the service of others.

Major events: Major school activities may be good occasions to gather school groups to celebrate the presence of Christ in his recreating power. Christ comes to restore all to dignity and beauty and calls all to be the sons and daughters of the loving Father. This call reaches forth and touches all of life. Penance celebrations give opportunities for Christ to be alive in the hearts and lives of his friends and loved ones.

Anniversaries: The anniversary of the school's dedication, the feast of the school's patron, and other significant events of school life are excellent occasions for penance celebrations within the school community. These celebrations may recall the need for forgiveness as the school members grow in service and care for one another.

Graduation: The time of graduation is both a time of departure and of new beginnings. To bid farewell to friends, companions, and memories, and to face the new and unknown world is part of Christ's approach to life. The forgiveness and peace of our Lord make this a rich step on the spiritual journey.

Class penance celebrations: The Canadian catechetical program gives many outlines for these celebrations. Following a catechesis on penance, a celebration may be held either in the school or in a parish setting. It is desirable to have the children involved in the planning and celebration of these services. (See *Rite of Penance*, Canadian edition, Appendix II, pages 139-142.)

Specific Groups

Religious communities: Christ has called some members of his Church to follow his Son more closely and to serve his people in a special way. Devoted to the service of many and called to give living witness to the future life, the lives of religious are uplifted and graced in penance celebrations. These celebrations may take place during the feasts of the community, anniversaries of profession, and during the high moments of the liturgical year.

Youth: Those involved in the ministry of youth are called to open the rich treasures of God's forgiving love for and with the young. The freedom from sin offered to those who are sons and daughters of the Father is heard in the invitation of Jesus to repentance. Youth should be assisted to be more generous in the service of friends and family. Through penance celebrations they will hear the word of God and in turn will be aided in their efforts to build the new earth and the new heavens in the spirit of gospel faith and love.

Ministries to the sick and elderly: Those involved in the ministry to the sick and elderly in hospitals and nursing homes are called to proclaim repentance. Conscious that penance is a gift to be accepted with gratitude, those involved in these ministries benefit when they come together as a group to have a penance celebration. These celebrations help to open their lives even more to God. Service to others will be given with humility, and will help all to grow in dignity and love.

Workers: Those engaged in the restoration of the temporal order have a special call from God to bring new life and the Spirit of the Lord to their places of work and recreation and to their family. The temporal order involves personal and family values, cultural and economic structures, institutions of government and global structures. Values have been placed in these through the creating hand of God. Everything has its primacy in God. (*Decree on the Apostolate of the Laity,* nos. 2, 5, 6, 7.)

Penance celebrations enable the design of God to be presented as the call to restore all things in his image and likeness. During these celebrations workers may examine their lives as co-creators with God in the temporal order.

Professions: God calls certain persons to the caring and serving professions (doctors, lawyers, social workers). Their ministry touches in particular ways the lives of those who require the physical, mental, and legal expertise offered by those trained in the healing and helping sciences. Sensitivity and generosity in the use of gifts and talents given by the creator are integral in these ministries.

Penance celebrations designed for these groups enable the living word to be present in its compassion, mercy, and hope. Christ's road to health and salvation reviewed at the time of these celebrations focuses on service for others in Christ.

Retreats and Missions

Retreats and days of recollection give the occasion to deepen one's Christian spirituality which has its origins in baptism. Baptism initiates one's life into the dying and rising of the Lord Jesus. The paschal mystery is the center of the Church's celebration (see Liturgy constitution, no. 6), and the center of the spiritual life. Baptism makes us sharers in the priesthood of Jesus Christ. It gives both the privilege and responsibility to be sharers in the priesthood (see 1 Pet. 2: 9-10) and the invitation to give him praise and thanks as we gather in his name.

Retreat time then is the time to realize once again that we die to Christ and are raised with him to share new life and to take part in his total victory over sin. We are his new creation. It is further the time to remind ourselves that we are signed in confirmation as witnesses of Christ to help in building up the kingdom.

Penance celebrations held during retreats and days of recollection help us to deepen our baptismal conversion. They may well provide the launching pad for some to celebrate the individual rite of reconciliation. Christ's victory over sin, which we first shared through baptism, is center stage in retreat penance celebrations.

Parish missions and days of renewal: During the time of a parish mission the parish family gathers to hear once more the gospel message present and alive in the Church. Time should be provided for reflection upon faith and on how one lives the Christian life. The paschal mystery is central to these days. The parish community celebrates this mystery and renews its life when it gathers to hear once more the living word of God.

The community is invited to examine its collective conscience. It looks at the root cause of disunity and how Jesus rescues his people from sin. Jesus is presented as the one who heals and restores all to the life of grace. He is the one who brings harmony and new strength for all to live a life of charity and justice in the marketplace of life.

These times give excellent possibilities for penance celebrations. The movement away from the afflictions of sin and to the burning love of Christ highlights these celebrations. The mission of the baptized to go forth and teach the gospel is the new challenge presented. Parishioners become aware that they are life-givers and light-bearers in all aspects of life. Special penance celebrations may be held for the sick and shut-ins, the elderly, the youth, and families during these days.

Family Events

Many opportunities are found within the family to celebrate God's merciful love and forgiveness.

Anniversaries: Birthdays and anniversaries (of baptism, confirmation, first eucharist, the death of a loved one) may be times of renewal, reflection and celebration. The Christian way of life is nourished and centered when family and friends gather to thank God for his blessings.

Penance celebrations may be planned by the family members and invitations to relatives and friends extended. Celebrations in which family life is reviewed help the family to discover how faith is lived both in word and deed. The graciousness and generosity of God is acknowledged. New efforts are undertaken to lead the life of dying to sin and living in grace.

Wedding anniversaries: The parish, which is made up of many families, gives praise and thanks to the Lord when families celebrate special anniversaries. The recognition of 25th and 50th anniversaries of marriage is a common practice in many areas. This is a special time of grace given to praise and thank God for long life and blessings in marriage and family life. The family lives the journey of the cross and resurrection in its many aspects of daily life. This is seen in moments of joy and sorrow, happiness and praise, birth and death.

Lived in the gospel spirit these moments are the fabric of holiness and the garment of love. The parish has special cause to call together those faithful to marriage over the years and ask that they renew and rededicate their energies once more to healthy family life.

It is opportune in this setting to plan a penance celebration on the faith life of the family. Family and friends may be invited to celebrate the gifts of mercy, peace, forgiveness, and hope which make possible family unity and love.

Happenings: Occasions such as a family member leaving home, time of sickness and suffering, the beginning of vacation, birthdays of grandparents, the beginning of a new job, involvement in community life are times in which a family may wish to have a penance celebration.

Family customs: Customs coming from a family's ethnic and cultural background may be considered as faith times. The family gathers to celebrate the mercy and ongoing forgiveness of God.

PREPARING A CELEBRATION

Elements
of a
penance celebration

Penance celebrations arc occasions when people gather to hear the word of God proclaimed. Through the proclaiming of the word they are invited to conversion and renewal of life. The death-resurrection of Jesus is the way to the overcoming of sin and the leading of the life of grace and freedom. In a fully developed celebration the following elements are normally found; depending upon the pastoral situation, some of these may be modified or omitted.

Theme

In developing the theme for the celebration it is important to consider:

• The liturgical season in which the celebration occurs;

• The readings from the word of God appropriate to the liturgical season or event being celebrated. Preferably the recommended readings in the *Rite of Penance*, nos. 101-201, are to be used.

This theme may be explained in a few sentences before the service begins, after the greeting, or in any leaflet distributed to the congregation.

Entrance Rite

1. Song: This song may be seasonal; or a hymn of praise; or a call to conversion. It should be one which is familiar to most of the people present.

See the liturgical index in the choir edition of CBW II, nos. 734-847: *Sacraments — penance, baptism; new creation, reconciliation with God, reconciliation with others; Holy Spirit, victory over sin and death, word of God, mercy of God; comfort and consolation, paschal mystery, thanksgiving.*

Other topics are suggested in the notes at the beginning of each season in CBW II, choir edition.

2. Enthroning the word of God: The book of God's word is carried in procession by the deacon or reader. The book is laid with reverence on the lectern, and opened. The candles are placed nearby. The presiding priest or leader incenses the book after it has been enthroned.

3. Greeting: After all make the sign of the cross, the president greets the assembled community. Sample greetings from the Fathers are included in the celebration outlines presented in this book, and scripture references to others are given; these may be adapted. It is desirable to rewrite them so that the people may answer with their customary *And also with you.*

The president or one of the assistants may explain the theme briefly, if this has not already been done.

4. Opening prayer: The president may choose a suitable prayer from the seasonal liturgy; or, one may be composed based on the theme developed in the readings chosen for this celebration. A model prayer is included in each of the celebrations in this book.

Liturgy of the Word

God's word invites us to conversion and renewal of our life by proclaiming that Christ's death and rising have freed us from slavery to sin, and have made us his people of praise.

One or more scripture readings may be proclaimed. If there is only one reading, it is taken from the gospel.

5. Reading from the word of God: The first reading may be chosen from the recommended readings in the *Rite of Penance,* the seasonal lectionary, or the scripture readings in the *Liturgy of the Hours.* Normally this reading is taken from the Old Testament, and in the Easter season from the Acts of the Apostles.

6. Meditative silence: A few moments of silence follow the reading, allowing all to reflect and pray in response to the word they have heard in faith. This silence is essential to enable each hearer to receive the word with the inner person. It gives time for the listener to accept the word and then respond with faith and hope.

7. Responsorial psalm: After the first reading and a pause for silent reflection, one of the responsorial psalms found in CBW II, nos. 110-337, may be chosen.

8. Second reading: If a second reading is used, it may be chosen from the New Testament readings recommended in the *Rite of Penance,* or from those in the seasonal lectionary, or in the *Liturgy of the Hours.*

● *Gospel acclamation:* See notes and references in CBW II, no. 86. (During Lent, *Alleluia* is not sung, and is replaced by another acclamation: nos. 359-364.)

9. Gospel reading: The person who reads the gospel may go in procession with candles and incense to the lectern. The book may be incensed and then the gospel is proclaimed.

● *Other readings* from the Church Fathers or others may be read before or after the scripture readings. The purpose of these readings is to help all to become more aware of sin and to have a deeper sorrow for it. (See *Rite of Penance,* no. 36.)

10. Homily: The president proclaims the wonderful works and mercy of God as revealed in the scripture texts, and leads the assembly to prayer for sinners, a reflective examination of conscience, and repentance.

11. Prayer for sinners: The entire Church prays for sinners, asking God in his mercy to bring them back to full life in his family; this should be particularly true throughout the lenten season. (See *Rite of Penance,* no. 8.)

During the penance celebration, the president should invite and encourage the congregation to pray for sinners: for themselves; for members of the community; and for sinners throughout the world (see 1 Jn. 5: 16). This prayer may well be backed up by an appeal for fasting by families, individuals, and the believing community.

12. Hymn: If desired a hymn may be sung.

Examination of Our Christian Living

13. Examination of our Christian living: Suitable time is necessary to enable those gathered to reflect upon their Christian living. The questions or suggestions for reflection should be read slowly; and a pause made for silent prayer and meditation after each question or series of points has been presented.

Several sets of examinations for Christian living are given on pages 99-141. The parish liturgy committee may develop others suited for the people gathered in celebration. Questions that disturb the community should not be omitted.

14. Silent prayer: For about five minutes, all remain in silence. Sitting or kneeling as they wish, they discuss their way of life with the Lord.

15. Community act of sorrow: In this prayer, the *Lord, have mercy* may be sung: see CBW II, nos. 83c, 338a, 339a, or 343a.

16. General intercessions: At this point, a hymn may be sung by the choir or by all; or general intercessions may be prayed, reflecting the theme and leading into the Lord's prayer (no. 17, below).

Conclusion of the Rite

17. Lord's prayer: This prayer is best sung by all, as at Mass. The president may prepare an introduction to this prayer based on the theme of the service.

18. Sacred action: The presiding priest or leader invites all to share the peace of Christ with one another. This may be done as at Sunday Mass, or less formally.

19. Invitation to the sacrament: When confessors are available, the president may invite the congregation to take part in the individual rite of reconciliation after the bible service has ended.

20. Blessing: The presiding priest or leader concludes the celebration with a blessing. Sample texts are found in each outline of this book.

21. Concluding hymn: At the conclusion of the celebration, all sing a seasonal hymn or song of praise or thanks.

Developing
a good
celebration

Good celebrations require adequate planning on the part of many in the Christian community. The atmosphere of prayer and reflection is essential to enable the word of God to be active and present in the lives of those who plan these celebrations. Before a parish liturgy committee commences planning it is suggested that they spend some time in prayer and reflection upon a selected scripture passage. A psalm, a hymn, moments of silence, and a brief reflection by a member of the planning committee will be helpful in approaching the actual planning.

The *Rite of Penance* provides several outlines for specific penitential services (Canadian edition, Appendix II, pages 113-152). As well, the rite gives an extensive list of scripture texts in nos. 101-201 (pages 86-94).

The parish liturgy committee should be encouraged to develop services that meet the spiritual needs of their community.

Purpose: The purpose of a penance celebration should be clear to the planning group. The celebration should:

- Foster the life of penance within the group

- Enable the word of God to be heard by the listeners

- Invite those gathered to conversion and renewed commitment to Christ's way of life

- Help prepare those gathered for individual reconciliation which takes place at a convenient time (see *Rite of Penance*, 37).

The planning committee should be conscious of the Church's hope for these celebrations. It should also be aware of the needs and expectations of the group for whom the celebration is being planned.

The liturgical season or feast or festival will help focus the specific theme for the celebration.

For whom: The planning committee is sensitive to the spiritual life of those who gather to celebrate. In planning these celebrations representatives from the group who will come together to celebrate may be invited to participate in the planning.[1]

---

[1] See the liturgical leaflet, *At Worship with the Disabled*, (1981, CCCB, Ottawa).

The Directory for Masses with Children[2] gives general principles for various types of celebrations. These may be helpful in planning penance celebrations with children.

Time: The time to hold these celebrations is decided upon in light of the availability of the parish or group to be present; the most conducive time for prayer and reflection; the readiness of the group to experience the loving forgiveness of Christ; and, the appropriate season or festive occasion.

Place: The place for the celebration is determined by the size of the group; the space suitable to create a reflective mood; the most suitable situation for creative expression, use of audio visuals, art and banners.

Approach: The approach taken in preparing a celebration may vary:

● The format outlined in this book, pages 21-23, may serve as a guide for planners. These outlines are in keeping with the suggestions found in the *Rite of Penance*, no. 36.

● This format may be adapted to the group celebrating. A parish celebration is normally more developed while a home celebration has a relaxed and informal flow.

● A parish planning group may develop its own format respecting the rhythm outlined in *Rite of Penance*, no. 36.

● A group with insufficient time to develop and plan a penance celebration may use one which is already developed. But they still need to accompany their planning with prayer and reflection.

Ministries: It is important to have as many as possible carry out specific ministries in these celebrations. These include the president or leader, the readers, the choir, musicians, servers, ushers, and those involved in creative expression.

Examination of conscience: An examination of conscience prepared by the planning committee is most desirable. The planning group is normally the group most familiar with the ebb and flow of the community they represent. Suggested examinations of conscience are presented in this book to serve as models to assist in preparing examinations (see pages 99-141).

Proclamation: The readings suggested are contained in the lectionary, and should be proclaimed from it or from a dignified bible. Canada's lectionary is richly bound to signify our respect for the scriptures and to emphasize the place of God's word in our spiritual growth. Scripture references, including the psalms, are from *The Jerusalem Bible*.

Participation: The Vatican Council suggests many ways of promoting active participation in liturgy: pastors are to encourage people to take part by their acclamations and responses, and by singing psalms, antiphons, and hymns, as well as by their actions and bodily postures. Reverent silence for reflection is an essential part of good participation (see Liturgy constitution, no. 30). An effort should be made to include all or many of these methods in these celebrations.

---

[2] The Directory for Masses with Children is contained in the introduction to the sacramentary. See the Canadian edition (1974, CCC, Ottawa), pages 55-64.

Full celebration: There should be a presiding priest or leader, the reader who carries the lectionary, servers (including two with lighted candles), crossbearer, thurifer, and choir. The president presides, leads the prayer, and preaches the message of conversion. This will be more effective when others are encouraged to assume their proper roles.

People's leaflet: Parishes may encourage the people to use the Canadian hymnal as their response book; others may wish to prepare leaflets to help their people take a full part in the psalms and responses. In small communities, *Sunday Mass Book* may be used.

Prayer and fasting: During the week before the penance celebration, members of the parish may be invited to prepare for it by prayer, fasting, and penance on one or more weekdays. By their communal prayer and fasting they will plead for God's mercy on sinners and help for all his people in this community (see Bulletin 42, pages 16-18).

New Testament and psalm books: In the week before the penance celebration, the parish bulletin may invite the people to bring their bible, New Testament, or psalm book for personal meditation before and after the celebration of the sacrament of reconciliation. Other copies may be placed in the pews.

Banners and posters based on the theme, or reflecting the spirit of the season, may help to set the mood for this celebration.

Creative expression such as mime, dance, dramatic reading, or use of light and sound may help the group to experience and celebrate the wonderful deeds of God's mercy and forgiveness, with greater faith, hope and love.

Who May Lead the Celebration?

Some think it strange to raise the question in the title of this article: it is evident that the priest is the leader of the penance celebration! This may be true in the average parish, but there are many other circumstances and situations in the Church today.

Penitential celebrations are recognized as helpful in situations where the priest is unavailable to give sacramental absolution. Such celebrations help people to have proper dispositions in moving from sin to grace, enable them to turn to God with true sorrow, and open the possibility for them to take part in sacramental absolution (see *Rite of Penance,* no. 37).

In keeping with this direction the following may be leaders of penance celebrations:

— priest in the parish
— retreat directors or leaders of renewal programs
— deacons or leaders of the Christian community
— catechists or teachers in the school and classroom
— chaplains or pastoral workers
   in hospitals and homes for the aged
— leaders of parish organizations and groups
— prayer leaders acceptable to the community
— parents in the family.

Parish leadership has the responsibility to train those who lead these celebrations. Areas to be considered in this formation include:

* the life of the baptized and implications for ministry
* the Christian community called to prayer
* the Christian community called to faith and conversion
* the celebrating community
* called to be a people of the Lord
* the word of God — essential for celebration
* ministries in penance celebrations
* practical helps for leaders of penance celebrations.

Further helps on the role of the leader in these celebrations may be found in the National Bulletin on Liturgy, no. 79, *Sunday Liturgy: When Lay People Preside* (May-June 1981).

Music In Celebrations

Why do we sing in the liturgy? Singing is a very human way of expressing our feelings: joy, elation, happiness, sorrow, sadness, sympathy. When we sing alone, and especially when we sing with others, we can be gathered up in our song, borne along by its rhythm and power, and our feelings are intensified.

Music and song are part of our liturgy because they are beautiful. They help us to become one in offering our entire selves to God in our prayer and worship.

Music and song are part of our baptismal spirituality: they are appropriate in our worship because we are Christians, chosen by God, chosen in Christ, set aside to sing God's praise. Jesus is the supreme song, the great psalmist, God's Word of praise and glory. Through Christ we continue to sing the Father's praise on earth. We give him glory for saving us through his Son's dying and rising. We praise God and thank him in the name of all creation. In our liturgy and in our personal prayer, we voice the praise of the universe, and unite our voices with the Church of heaven.

We sing and dance and play music in the liturgy because God is so great and because in baptism he has made us his holy people of praise.

Prayerful music: Liturgy is prayer: we join with Jesus in *praising* God and in *praying* for the world. The music we use — songs, melodies, dance, and other gestures — must therefore be prayerful: leading us to praise and prayer, and helping us to praise and pray better.

Our music must encourage us to pray better, channelling our feelings and sentiments into harmony with our words and actions in the liturgy. Our music must be in tune with the spirit of the liturgy, and help us to be so too: in love with God and his people, eager to promote his kingdom of justice and peace, ready to serve as Christ served.

In the liturgy, music is not an escape from the reality of life, but rather a way of facing it more fully and of seeing it more clearly.

Prayerful music in prayerful liturgy is a foretaste of the heavenly liturgy, when we shall be one with Mary and the angels and the saints in offering our unending praise to the Father through the Son in the Holy Spirit.

Pastoral music: The Second Vatican Council returned the liturgy to the entire people of God. Before the Council the liturgy had become a sacred drama performed by selected persons, with the congregation serving as a passive audience. Since the Council, the liturgy is seen once more as the action of the whole Church. No one is an idle spectator, there is no audience; all are celebrants.

- *Assembly:* The group which celebrates the liturgy is the whole assembly — all the baptized Catholics gathered here and now — in union with the entire Church on earth and in heaven. The song of the whole community has first place in importance. Choir, cantor, and musicians, as well as priest, deacon, and other ministers, are part of this assembly, and work to support and uplift its song and its worship.

Music and song are pastoral when they contribute to the active participation of the whole assembly in the act of worship.

Faith and music: Music reflects the beauty, harmony, glory, and perfection of God. In his goodness, the Spirit has given the gift of music to many people. Those involved in the ministry of music need to be persons who believe and pray. Their public worship and their music should flow from their deep faith, from their daily lives, and from their personal prayer.

Musical excellence: In every parish and group, there are persons of God-given talent. The parish has the responsibility to discern the needs and gifts of the people, so that worthy worship may be offered to God by the community.

There is the need for each minister to strive for excellence in order to help all in their efforts to turn from sin and return to God. The quality of music used in penance celebrations will help all to be a people of prayer and hope.

Music in penance celebrations: Music is an important element in communal celebrations of forgiveness. The music chosen should reflect not only the need for mercy and forgiveness but also the mood of joy, thanksgiving, and renewed commitment which the community celebrates on such occasions.

Guidance for the use of music during penance celebrations and for the second and third rites of the sacrament is found in CBW II, nos. 29-32.

Other suggestions are found in the liturgical index of CBW II under these headings: *Sacraments — penance, baptism; new creation, reconciliation with others, Holy Spirit, victory over sin and death, word of God, mercy of God, comfort and consolation, paschal mystery, thanksgiving.*

Liturgy of the word

The liturgy of the word is an essential part of any penance celebration. A good celebration of the word leads the assembled Christians into a fuller and more fruitful participation in penance celebrations.

Outline: The readings and the homily proclaim God's word to his people, and they respond to it in silence, song, and prayer. The elements of the liturgy of the word are celebrated in this sequence:

* *First reading,* silent prayer, responsorial psalm
* *Second reading,* silent prayer
* *Gospel acclamation,* leading to the third reading
* *Gospel,* silent prayer
* *Homily,* silent prayer
* *Prayer for the Church and the world.*

God Is Present and Speaking to Us

A deeper dimension: The dynamics of proclaiming God's word in faith to his assembled people go far beyond the rules for good public reading. In liturgical celebrations, the reading becomes an appearance of God among his people. He is present, and he is speaking to them — to this particular group in this town, as well as to each individual congregation and community around the world. It is not just a general message to all: in his infinite wisdom, the Spirit is ready to guide those who are open, so that the message has a personal as well as community impact.

● *Listening in faith:* Everyone in the baptized community is called to hear God's word with faith: the *ephphetha* rite over the ears during our baptism symbolizes our privilege and responsibility of hearing God's word. When the writer was inspired to set down the passages being read, the Spirit of God knew that they would be proclaimed on this day to this particular assembly. He invites us to open our hearts to the fullness of his teaching: we have prayed the introductory rites; we now sit in silence and let the word of God flow over us, washing into the depths of our being. We allow the Spirit to enlighten our darkness, to cool our uncontrolled desires, to warm our coldness, to bend our rigid ways.

● *Proclaiming in faith:* The entire assembly is called to listen to the word. Some members of the community are also invited to share in the great responsibility of proclaiming the word so that all may listen to it with faith: the readers who proclaim the first two readings, the leader who reads the gospel, and the one who preaches the homily.

These persons are called to be the *voice of God* in this celebration. They indeed read the words of scripture and give the homily, but always in such a way that God's voice comes through to those who listen: the voice may be the voice of Jacob or Ms. Jacob, but the message is the message of God.

Proclaiming the Word of God

Introduction: The leader may give a brief introduction to the readings. This is particularly beneficial when one of the readings seems difficult before its context is understood.

First reading: The first reading is chosen in relation to the gospel passage and is therefore best understood when seen in this light.

Some thoughts for the person who proclaims the first reading:

• *Going to the lectern:* As the people are sitting down after the opening prayer, the reader moves quietly to the lectern. The readers should always sit near the lectern so that they do not have to cross the sanctuary. On arrival, the reader waits for all to settle down; if the leader makes a brief introduction to the readings at this point, the reader listens with the rest of the community. Then he or she may bow slightly to the leader, face the people, and begin to read.

• *Reading from the lectionary:* Each reader should proclaim the word of God from the lectionary or an approved version of the scriptures.[1]

• *Title:* The reader reads what is printed in black in the lectionary: "A reading from the book of Exodus." There is no need for added words or information: title, scripture references, summary line, or "Our first reading today is taken from . . . ."

• *Reading:* The text is read as given in the lectionary or bible. The decision to use a longer or shorter passage depends on the circumstances of the celebration and the community's ability to benefit from the passage chosen. This decision should be made in advance. Readers should make sure they are comfortable with both the meaning and the pronunciation of all the words in the title and the reading.

• *End of the reading:* On coming to the end of the reading, the reader should stop, look the people in the eye, pause, and then proclaim: *This is the word of the Lord!* When the reader says this well, the people will respond with a firm acclamation, *Thanks be to God!*

Pause for silent prayer: When God's word has been proclaimed, a period of silent reflection is called for, so that the Spirit may speak to each of us. Particularly in today's liturgy of the word, silence is needed if the scriptures are to penetrate more deeply into our hearts and our lives.

After the people's response to the readings, the reader remains standing at the lectern, facing the people with head bowed: this will be a sign for all to pause for silent reflection and prayer. We may think about some action, advice, or phrase in the reading, or simply ask the Spirit to open our hearts to his grace-filled action. Or we may echo Christ's response, and simply pray: *Here I am, Father: I am ready to do your will* (see Heb. 10: 7 and Ps. 40: 7-8).

• *Introducing the time of silent prayer:* In parishes where this silent pause has not been observed, it may be introduced gradually. Perhaps a 20-second pause will be adequate as a beginning; in the months to come, as the community learns to pray in silence, this may be increased gradually.

---

[1] *The Jerusalem Bible,* the *New American Bible,* and the *Revised Standard Version* are approved for liturgical use in Canada.

Responsorial psalm: Reader, singers, and people remain in silent reflection for a moment after the first reading. After this time of personal prayer, we continue our response to God's action by playing the responsorial psalm.

The psalm and its refrain are chosen to reflect and respond to the first reading, which in turn is closely related to the gospel. The refrain is a prayer on which all may reflect following the celebration.

The responsorial psalm should be sung whenever possible. CBW II provides a sung refrain and an appropriate psalm tone for many of the psalms. The psalm is sung in this way: the cantor (choir) sings the refrain, and all repeat it; the cantor (choir) sings the verse, and all repeat the refrain. This is continued until the last verse is sung and the refrain is repeated.

If a congregation is unable to find a cantor to sing the psalm text, the community may sing the seasonal refrain, with someone (probably the first reader) reading the verses of the seasonal psalm.

The least developed form is the one which is still used in many churches: one person (usually the reader) says the refrain, and all repeat it. He or she reads the verse, and all repeat the refrain. This dialogue continues until the last verse and the refrain are read.

Second reading: Where possible, another reader proclaims the second reading: this is considered better than having one person read both lessons and the psalm. A variety of well-prepared readers leads to a much better proclamation of the word.

• *Method:* The notes on the first reading (page 30) apply also to the second reading.

• *Silence:* At the end of the second reading, a pause for silent prayer is needed.

• If the reading of the gospel is from a special book of the gospels (which is on the altar), the reader takes the lectionary to the credence after the *Alleluia* begins.

Gospel acclamation: After the pause for silent prayer which follows the second reading, the whole atmosphere changes. We have been listening to the Father as he speaks to us. Now, with the gospel acclamation, we are preparing to listen to Jesus Christ, our brother, whom the Father has sent to speak to us directly. Several distinct elements are involved in this rite:

• *Posture:* We stand as a community to show that we are ready to greet Jesus and hear him speaking to us.

• *Acclamation:* The acclamation is addressed to Christ, as are the responses before and after the gospel reading.

• *Alleluia is for singing:* The gospel acclamation is intended to be sung by the whole community: it is our greeting and welcome — a standing ovation, as it were — to the Lord Jesus, who speaks to all in the gospel.

Gospel reading: The gospel text is the most important of the three readings proclaimed.

• *Procession:* The gospel acclamation is a greeting addressed to Jesus Christ. It is sung as the gospel book is carried in the procession to the place of the word, where the gospel is proclaimed with solemnity.

- *Signs of respect:* Acolytes carry lighted candles, and the thurifer carries burning incense to show the importance of the gospel. We mark the sign of the cross on our forehead, lips, and heart as we prepare to listen to Jesus. The gospel book is incensed as a symbol of the presence of Christ among us. At the end of the reading, the book may be held up for all to see and the leader declares that this is indeed the Lord's gospel. Then the book is kissed as a further sign of respect for our savior.

- *Place of proclamation:* The gospel is proclaimed from the same lectern as the first two readings. The one who reads the gospel always uses the lectionary or a bible — rather than a leaflet or loose page — to show the community's reverence for the word of Christ.

Preaching the Word

The homily: The gospels frequently present Jesus as the one who teaches the people and his disciples by preaching on various occasions. In Lk. 4: 16-30, we see him in the synagogue, where he preaches on the fulfillment of Is. 61: 1-2. Timothy is encouraged to preach in season and out (2 Tim. 4: 1-5).

Purpose: The primary purpose of preaching during the liturgy of the word is the *continuing conversion* of the people who hear the word. The homily is not exegesis, but is based on it. It is not so much instruction as reflection. It is a sharing of the leader's prayerful reflection on the word and on the life of the Spirit in this worshipping community.

The homily, based on the readings and other liturgical texts and actions, is the way in which the presider bridges the gap between the living scriptures and the lives of today's people. The Spirit who inspired the biblical writings continues to be active in the community. The one who gives the homily must be open to the action of the Spirit, and co-operate with him to bring God's loving word into the hearts and lives of his people today.

Homily and readings: The homily is based principally on the scriptures and on the actions and texts of the liturgy (Liturgy constitution, nos. 52 and 35: 2). In the homily, God's wonderful works in the history of salvation are proclaimed, and the principles which guide the lives of Christians (Liturgy constitution, no. 52). The preacher shows God's people how the mystery of Christ continues to be present and active among us. By exploring some aspect of the scripture readings or of a text, this gathered community of God's people benefits more fully from the richness of his word and his other gifts in creation and in grace.

Homily and life: Through leading people to conversion and to self-offering, the homily prepares people to live their lives more in the spirit of the gospel message. With the rest of the assembled community, the presider listens to the word, and then shares prayerful reflections on what has been proclaimed. If in tune with the pastoral circumstances and needs of the people of this parish, the presider is able to help the people understand their way of life in the light of the gospel: people today listen "more willingly to witnesses than to teachers."[2]

---

[2] See Paul VI, *On Evangelization in the Modern World, Evangelii nuntiandi,* December 8, 1975 (1976, USCC, 1312 Massachusetts Ave. NW, Washington, DC 20005): no. 41.

Open book: It is more desirable to preach the word from the open book as a clear sign that it is the Lord's word which is being shared in the homily: such a sign speaks loudly.

*　　*　　*

Following the homily the community is invited to pray for the Church and the world. A prayer for sinners may be included in these petitions (see page 23).

PSALMS

Praying the psalms: There are many opportunities for using the psalms in the revised rites. [Numbers in this paragraph refer to the 1973 *Rite of Penance.*] In community celebrations, psalms may be used as the entrance song (no. 48), responsorial psalm (51), proclamation of praise (56, 206), and concluding song; when general absolution is given, the act of penance or satisfaction (60) may be a psalm. In the reconciliation of an individual, both priest and penitent may pray one or more psalms as they prepare (15). The invitation to trust in God (42), reading from his word (43), act of satisfaction (6c, 44), prayer of sorrow (45, 85, 86), and proclamation of praise (47, 206) may be chosen from the psalms. Suitable psalms are listed in the *Rite,* nos. 133-147, and 206.

Psalms need not be used in all these instances, of course, but the opportunities are there to be explored. An occasional praying of the penitential psalms helps us to retain an abiding sorrow for our sins.

Penitential psalms: The Church encourages us to pray for sinners, beginning with ourselves. We may use the penitential psalms in this way. In words inspired by the Holy Spirit, we ask God for his mercy and pardon for ourselves and all the world.

From the sixth century, seven psalms were seen as particularly appropriate for use by penitents: These are Psalms 6, 32, 38, 51, 102, 130, and 143. Innocent III (1198-1216) commanded that they should be prayed during Lent. In the reform of the office of St. Pius X, the penitential psalms became part of the lenten office for Fridays. They are no longer included in the present form of the liturgy of the hours, but may be considered as suitable for prayer in Lent; during a penance celebration or when preparing for the sacrament of reconciliation; and on days of fast, retreat, or renewal.

Suggestions for a prayerful celebration

Preparation

Preparing the community for prayer: The Church is always holy, and yet "always in the need of being purified," as it constantly follows "the path of penance and renewal" (Constitution on the Church, no. 8).

When it comes together in worship, the Church is in a posture of prayer. The Church gives thanks and praise for the Father's great love for us, his creation, and saving action in Jesus the Lord. The need constantly exists to pray for the Church, for all members of the Church: parents and children; ministers of the gospel; all categories and types of believers; the strong and the weak; those who struggle with sin and those who are living in Christ.

The invitation extended in the parish bulletin to come and take part in a penance celebration should remind all of the importance of prayer and penance in life. The parish may be invited to pray for sinners. They may also be reminded that they are called to share daily in the cross of Christ and to make up by penance what is lacking in the suffering of Christ.

In the time before a penance celebration, the parish members should be encouraged to pray that many will be touched by the forgiving love of Christ. Scripture passages centered on the words and life of Jesus made available to the parish allow prayerful reflection to take place. This is a valuable time to consider the true significance of sin and to realize that the call to conversion is extended to all.

Preparing the ministers for prayer: Those who fulfill ministries such as reader, musician, and cantor should come together in prayer prior to the actual celebration. This time spent together in prayer will help the leaders of the celebration to be of one heart and mind in approaching and leading the celebration. Those who exercise the various ministries within the celebration will be aware of the flow of the entire celebration and unity among the various elements (readings, music, hospitality) will exist.

Provisions should be made for the leaders of these celebrations to have ample time to reflect upon the word of God, and to consider the place of penance in the life of the Church. Involvement by the leaders in the planning of these celebrations will open the rich spiritual treasuries to all who seek inner harmony and peace.

Other suggestions: To help develop a penitential spirit within the community, other privileged acts of penance are recommended. These forms are considered privileged because they are based on the teaching of the gospel or because of their traditional value among the people of God.

• *Christian fasting* obtains its full measure when we deprive ourselves of food in order to be more open to prayer, to share more fully in the suffering of those who are starving, and to save money to give to the poor. Fasting among Christians is a penitential discipline turning our hearts to God and others, a means of purification and spiritual liberation, and a witness to the depths of our faith.

• *Works of mercy* done in the spirit of Christ enable the building up of the kingdom to happen. To recognize that many in today's world search for meaning and help in life gives courage to the believing community in its care, love and service of one another. It is by lived faith both in word and deed that one's life becomes the gospel to others.

Gathered to Celebrate

A faith-filled and prayerful celebration builds up and expresses the presence of Christ in the community. In the celebration these considerations are important:

Beginning: Those involved in the celebration prepare for their participation by moments spent in silent recollection calling to mind that they are the servants of the word of God. They ask the Holy Spirit to be with them in the exercise of their ministry within the celebration.

Entrance: In a full celebration an entrance procession is arranged. It is accompanied by the entrance song as the ministers and leader proceed to the sanctuary.

Sign of the cross: Once all have arrived at their places, the leader begins with the sign of the cross and all answer *Amen.* This gesture made with care and respect professes faith in the Father, Son, and Holy Spirit.

Greeting: The liturgical greeting is a reminder to all that Christ is present among us. Various suggestions for this greeting are found in the penance celebrations of this book.

Opening prayer: The leader invites all to pray with the simple *Let us pray* or a slightly expanded invitation. A pause for a time of silence then takes place. This gives time to remember we are in God's presence as well as an opportunity for personal petitions. Then the leader continues and offers the prayer of the community *to* the Father, *through* the Son, and *in* the Spirit.

Liturgy of the word: see pages 29-33.

Examination of our Christian living: In many ways this is at the heart of the celebration. Having heard the word of God and its call to conversion those gathered place themselves in a mood of prayerful reflection. In the spirit of prayer the examination of conscience or review of Christian living is undertaken. Again the inspiration for this examination comes from the word of God and is developed in the context of lived faith. The examination ideally should be adapted to the needs of the gathered group. Two readers may alternate in presenting the points for reflection. Adequate pauses should be allowed to enable reflection to be realized.

Community act of sorrow: Following the examination the community expresses heartfelt sorrow for its sinfulness and expresses its resolution to live for God. This act of solidarity aids the community and individuals within the community to be aware of the truth that it is Christ who enlightens the inner person and grants strength to be more Christlike to all aspects of life. (See Colossians 1: 21-23.)

Conclusion of the rite: The Lord's prayer has first place in the concluding rite. Again God is acclaimed as *Our Father.* He is the one who sends Jesus among us as savior, the one who brings the gift of loving forgiveness to all who come to him in faith. The petition *forgive us as we forgive those who trespass against us* asks that we be one in heart and mind, one with self, others and God.

Following the Lord's prayer members of the assembled community are invited to extend a gesture of peace to one another. This act of reaching out to express the inner peace of the heart has great meaning at this moment. It represents the exterior expression of the new peace that is experienced in the inner person.

In penance celebrations people gather to hear the word of God proclaimed. They are invited by the power of God's word to change their lives from sin and to the life of grace. Jesus, through his death and resurrection, shows the way to overcome sin and to live for God.

The outlines for penance celebrations presented in this book are provided to help the Christian community in its efforts to die to sin and live for God. When celebrated in faith and the spirit of prayer, these celebrations will open up the possibility for the celebration of the individual rite of reconciliation.

CELEBRATION OUTLINES

Fifteen celebration outlines are presented in this section of the book (see pages 38-97). These outlines are intended to provide help to those who plan and lead penance celebrations. They may be adapted to the needs of the local parish or group who gather to celebrate God's forgiveness and mercy. The suggestions for the readings, music, and prayers take advantage of the rich treasures found in the Canadian family of liturgical books.

Readings: Many of the suggested readings may be found in the Canadian lectionaries. Reference numbers 1-175 are found in the *Lectionary for Mass*, Sunday edition; numbers 176-926 are found in *Lectionary for Mass*, weekday edition.

It is recommended that the readers use either the lectionary or bible to proclaim the readings during these celebrations. The *Jerusalem Bible*, the *New American Bible*, and the *Revised Standard Version* are approved for liturgical use in Canada.

Music: Guidance for the use of music during penance celebrations is found in CBW II, nos. 29-32, and in the liturgical index. Further suggestions on the place of music in penance celebrations are found on pages 27-28 of this book.

Other resources:

● *The Rite of Penance,* Canadian edition, contains many celebration outlines and suggested scripture readings.

● The Canadian catechetical program offers valuable help for penance celebrations at the various grade levels.

CELEBRATION OUTLINES

CALLED TO GIVE PRAISE AND THANKS

Entrance Rite

1. Song

2. Enthroning the word of God

3. Greeting: After all make the sign of the cross, the president greets the assembled community with one of the following, adapted as necessary:

2 Thess. 3: 18
Heb. 13: 25a

or the following greeting from St. Ignatius of Antioch:

**All happiness to you
in God the Father and in Jesus Christ.**

And also with you.

4. Opening prayer: The president may choose a suitable prayer from the sacramentary; or one may be composed, based on the theme developed in the readings chosen for this celebration. One example of this prayer:

**Let us pray to God our Father,
and praise him for choosing us in Christ
as his beloved people of praise.**

All pause for silent prayer.

**Blessed are you, Father of all,
ruler of the universe:
you have loved us so fully
that you sent your Son to save us.**

**Before time began, you chose us in him
to be your holy people, blameless in your sight.
You have called us to sing your praises
by our works and by our words
until all people are drawn to give you glory.**

**We praise you for saving us from sin
and for making us your beloved people.**

**Help us to turn from sin
and give you praise by our good works,
and so lead others to your love.**

**All glory and praise are yours, Father,
for ever and ever.**

Liturgy of the Word

God's word invites us to conversion and renewal of our life by proclaiming that Christ's death and rising have freed us from slavery to sin, and have made us his people of praise.

5. Reading from the word of God: The first reading may be chosen from:

Eph. 1: 3-14	lectionary, no. 105
1 Pet. 2: 4-9	no. 53
Titus 2: 11-14	no. 14

6. Meditative silence: A few moments of silence follow the reading, allowing all to reflect and pray in response to the word they have heard in faith.

7. Psalm: After silent prayer, a psalm or hymn is sung.

8. Second reading: If a second reading is used, it may be chosen from one of the New Testament texts above, or from readings in the seasonal lectionary. A moment of silent prayer follows this reading.

A gospel acclamation may be chosen from CBW II.

9. Gospel reading:

Mt. 5: 1-12a	lectionary, no. 71
Lk. 11: 1-13	no. 112

10. Homily: The president proclaims the wonderful works and mercy of God as revealed in the scripture texts, and leads the assembly to prayer for sinners, to a reflective examination of conscience, and to repentance.

11. Prayer for sinners: The leader invites all to pray:

**Let us pray for sinners
and ask God to forgive them:**

All pause for silent prayer.

**Heavenly Father,
you do not want sinners to die,
but to live in grace and serve you in love.
Look upon the people of the world
and draw them back to you through Christ.**

**With him we pray:
Father, forgive them, for they know not what they do!**

**Send your Spirit to soften hard hearts,
to bend rigid wills,
to warm those who are indifferent to you,
and to lead them to give you praise.**

Father,
forgive us our sins
and listen to our prayers for all sinners.
Bring them back to your love through our example,
so that with them we may praise you
and celebrate our thanks through Christ our Lord.

12. Hymn: If desired, a hymn may be sung.

Examination of Christian Living

13. Examination of conscience: See pages 99-141.

14. Silent prayer: For about five minutes, all remain in silence. Sitting or kneeling as they wish, they discuss their way of life with the Lord.

15. Community act of sorrow:

Reader or president:
Lord, you have taught us to be the light of the world:
forgive us for failing to be people of light.
Lord, have mercy.

All: *Lord, have mercy.*

Christ, you have called us to be the people of love:
forgive us for choosing hatred and sin.
Christ, have mercy.

All: *Christ, have mercy.*

Lord, you have chosen us to do good,
to serve others in your Spirit of love:
forgive us for preferring to serve ourselves.
Lord, have mercy.

All: *Lord, have mercy.*

16. Acclamation: A hymn may be sung.

Or a brief form of the general intercessions may be based on the theme, ending with the Lord's prayer (no. 17).

Conclusion of the Rite

17. Lord's prayer: This prayer is best sung by all. The president may prepare an introduction to this prayer, based on the theme of the service. For example:

God has called us to be his people of praise.
Let us pray with Jesus to our Father:

Our Father . . .

18. Sacred action: The leader invites all to share the peace of Christ with one another, and introduces the rite in this way:

Jesus gives his forgiveness and peace
to all the people of God.
Let us share his peace and love with one another.

19. Invitation to the sacrament: The president may invite the congregation to celebrate the sacrament of penance after the bible service has ended.

20. Blessing: The leader may conclude with a simple blessing, or may use this form:

May the Father of light bless you with all good,
and protect you from all evil.

All: *Amen!*

May his wisdom enlighten your hearts,
and give you everlasting understanding.

All: *Amen!*

May he look upon you with mercy,
and raise you to unending happiness.

All: *Amen!*

May our all-powerful God
— the Father, the + Son, and the Holy Spirit —
bless you and keep you for ever.

All: *Amen!*

21. Concluding hymn: All sing a seasonal hymn or song of praise.

NOT MY WILL, BUT YOURS BE DONE

Entrance Rite

1. Song

2. Enthroning the word of God

3. Greeting: After all make the sign of the cross, the president greets the assembled community with one of the following, adapted as necessary:

    1 Tim. 1: 2b
    1 Tim. 6: 21b

or the following greeting from St. Ignatius of Antioch:

**May all happiness be with you
in purity of spirit
and in the word of God.**

And also with you.

4. Opening prayer: The president may choose a suitable prayer from the sacramentary; or one may be composed, based on the theme developed in the readings chosen for this celebration. One example of this prayer:

**Let us pray to God our Father,
and ask for the grace to obey his will for us.**

All pause for silent prayer.

**All praise to you, Father of all, ruler of the universe:
you have loved us so fully
that you sent your Son to save us.
In obedience to your will
he accepted death on the cross,
and you raised him in glory to give us new life.**

**Help us to turn away from sin and follow him in love,
ready to listen to your Spirit
and eager to do your will.**

**All glory and praise are yours, Father,
for ever and ever.**

Liturgy of the Word

God's word invites us to conversion and renewal of our life by proclaiming the Good News: by his death and rising, Christ has freed us from slavery to sin, and has made it possible for us to live for God.

5. Reading from the word of God: The first reading may be chosen from:

Eph. 5: 8-14	lectionary, no. 31
Eph. 5: 15-20	no. 120
Heb. 4: 14-16; 5: 7-9	no. 41
1 Jn. 2: 1-5	no. 48

6. Meditative silence: A few moments of silence follow the reading, allowing all to reflect and pray in response to the word they have heard in faith.

7. Psalm: After silent prayer, a psalm or hymn is sung.

8. Second reading: If a second reading is used, it may be chosen from one of the New Testament texts above, or from readings in the seasonal lectionary. A moment of silent prayer follows this reading.

A gospel acclamation may be chosen from CBW II.

9. Gospel reading:

Mk. 14: 32-42	to be selected
Mt. 26: 36-46	from the passion
Lk. 22: 39-46	narratives, no. 38;
Mt. 21: 28-32	no. 137

10. Homily: The president proclaims the wonderful works and mercy of God as revealed in the scripture texts, and leads the assembly to prayer for sinners, to a reflective examination of conscience, and to repentance.

11. Prayer for sinners: The leader invites all to pray:

**Let us pray for sinners
and ask God to forgive them:**

All pause for silent prayer.

**Heavenly Father,
you do not want sinners to die,
but to live in grace and serve you in love.
Look upon the people of the world
and draw them back to you through Christ.**

With him we pray:

**Father, forgive them, for they know not what they do!
Send your Spirit to soften hard hearts,
to bend rigid wills
and to warm those who are indifferent to you.**

**Father, forgive us our sins
and listen to our prayers for all sinners.
Bring them back to your love through our example,
so that with them we may praise you
and celebrate our thanks through Christ our Lord.**

12. Hymn: If desired, a hymn may be sung.

Examination of Christian Living

13. Examination of conscience: See pages 99-141.

14. Silent prayer: For about five minutes, all remain in silence. Sitting or kneeling as they wish, they discuss their way of life with the Lord.

15. Community act of sorrow:

Reader or president:
Lord, you came to do the Father's will:
help us to follow you in obeying him.
Lord, have mercy.

All: *Lord, have mercy.*

Christ, you have taught us to do the will of the Father:
forgive us for the times we preferred to do our own.
Christ, have mercy.

All: *Christ, have mercy.*

Lord, you have made us children of the Father:
teach us to follow you in love and obedience.
Lord, have mercy.

All: *Lord, have mercy.*

16. Acclamation: A hymn may be sung.

Or a brief form of the general intercessions may be based on the theme, ending with the Lord's prayer (no. 17).

Conclusion of the Rite

17. Lord's Prayer: This prayer is best sung by all. The president may prepare an introduction to this prayer, based on the theme of the service. For example:

God has taught us to love one another.
Let us ask our Father in heaven
to help us to do his will on earth:

Our Father . . . .

18. Sacred action: The leader invites all to share the peace of Christ with one another, and introduces the rite in this way.

Jesus gives his forgiveness and peace
to those who do God's will.
Let us share his peace and love with one another.

19. Invitation to the sacrament: The president may invite the congregation to celebrate the sacrament of penance after the bible service has ended.

20. Blessing: The leader may conclude with a simple blessing, or may use this form:

May the Father, who has reconciled us in his love,
continue to shower his blessings upon us.

All: *Amen!*

May the Son, who died and rose to save us,
forgive us our sins
and help us to love one another more.

All: *Amen!*

May the Holy Spirit of God,
who makes us his temples of love and praise,
give us unending joy and peace.

All: *Amen!*

May almighty God,
Father, Son, + and Holy Spirit,
give you his blessing for ever and ever.

All: *Amen!*

21. Concluding hymn: All sing a seasonal hymn or song of praise.

WE ARE THE LIGHT OF THE WORLD

Entrance Rite

1. **Song**

2. **Enthroning the word of God**

3. Greeting: After all make the sign of the cross, the president greets the assembled community with one of the following, adapted as necessary:

> Col. 4: 18
> Gal. 1: 3

or the following greeting from the *Epistle of Barnabas:*

Greetings to you,
and peace in the name of the Lord Jesus who loves us.

And also with you.

4. Opening prayer: The president may choose a suitable prayer from the sacramentary; or one may be composed, based on the theme developed in the readings chosen for this celebration. One example of this prayer:

Let us pray to God our Father,
and praise him for choosing us in Christ
to be the light of the world.

All pause for silent prayer.

Blessed are you, Father of all,
ruler of the universe:
you have loved us so fully
that you sent your Son to save us.

He loved us and gave his life for us,
dying so that we might die to sin,
rising in order to raise us to life in you.

He is light from light,
and overcomes the darkness of sin.

We praise you for saving us from sin
and for making us your beloved people.

Help us to be the light of the world,
to give you praise by our good works,
and so lead others to praise you.

All glory and praise are yours, Father,
for ever and ever.

Liturgy of the Word

God's word invites us to conversion and renewal of our life by proclaiming that Christ's death and rising have freed us from the darkness of sin, and have brought us into the kingdom of light.

5. Readings from the word of God: The first reading may be chosen from:

Rom. 13: 11-14	lectionary, no. 1
Eph. 5: 8-14	no. 31
1 Thess. 5: 1-6, 9-11	no. 432

6. Meditative silence: A few moments of silence follow the reading, allowing all to reflect and pray in response to the word they have heard in faith.

7. Psalm: After silent prayer, a psalm or hymn is sung.

8. Second reading: If a second reading is used, it may be chosen from one of the New Testament texts above, or from readings in the seasonal lectionary. A moment of silent prayer follows this reading.

A gospel acclamation may be chosen from CBW II.

9. Gospel reading:

Mt. 5: 13-16 *Light on lampstand*	lectionary, no. 74
Jn. 1: 1-5, 9-14 (shorter reading) *1-9 In the beginning...*	no. 16
Jn. 9: 35-41 *the blind to see --- light comes into the world* Jn
Jn. 12: 32-36 *not the light.*

Walk in light while light is among you; who walks in darkness does not know where he's going

10. Homily: The president proclaims the wonderful works and mercy of God as revealed in the scripture texts, and leads the assembly to prayer for sinners, to a reflective examination of conscience, and to repentance.

11. Prayer for sinners: The leader invites all to pray:

Let us pray for sinners *us*
and ask God to forgive them.

All pause for silent prayer

Heavenly Father,
you do not want sinners to die,
but to live in grace and serve you in love.
Look upon the people of the world
and draw them back to you through Christ.
With him we pray:
Father, forgive them, for they know not what they do!

Send your Spirit to soften hard hearts,
to bend rigid wills,
to warm those who are indifferent to you,
and to bring your light into their lives.

Father, forgive us our sins
and listen to our prayers for all sinners.
Bring them back to your love through our example,
so that with them we may praise you
and celebrate our thanks through Christ our Lord.

12. Hymn: If desired, a hymn may be sung.

Examination of Christian Living

13. Examination of conscience: See pages 99-141.

14. Silent prayer: For about five minutes, all remain in silence. Sitting or kneeling as they wish, they discuss their way of life with the Lord.

15. Community act of sorrow:

Reader or president:
God has called us to be his people,
and has saved us through Jesus.
Let us pray to our Lord and ask his help.

Son of God and king of glory:
Lord, have mercy.

All: *Lord, have mercy.*

Savior of all and Lord of nations:
Christ, have mercy.

All: *Christ, have mercy.*

Jesus, our brother and our Lord:
Lord, have mercy.

All: *Lord, have mercy.*

16. Acclamation: A hymn may be sung.

Or a brief form of the general intercessions may be based on the theme, ending with the Lord's prayer (no. 17).

Conclusion of the Rite

17. Lord's prayer: This prayer is best sung by all, as at Mass. The president may prepare an introduction to this prayer, based on the theme of the service. For example:

God has given us his Son
to make us the people of light.
Let us pray with Jesus to our Father:

Our Father . . . .

18. Sacred action: The leader invites all to share the peace of Christ with one another, and introduces the rite in this way.

**Jesus gives his forgiveness and peace
to all the people of God.
Let us share his peace and love with one another.**

19. Invitation to the sacrament: The leader may invite the congregation to celebrate the sacrament of penance after the bible service has ended.

20. Blessing: The leader may conclude with a simple blessing, or may use this form:

**May the Father of light bless you with all good,
and protect you from all evil.**

All: *Amen!*

**May his wisdom enlighten your hearts,
and give you everlasting understanding.**

All: *Amen!*

**May he look upon you with mercy,
and raise you to unending happiness.**

All: *Amen!*

**May you be protected and blessed,
and made strong in faith, hope, and love
by our all-powerful and loving God,
the Father, the + Son, and the Holy Spirit.**

All: *Amen!*

21. Concluding hymn: All sing a seasonal hymn or song of praise.

WAITING IN HOPE

Entrance Rite

1. Song

2. Enthroning the word of God

3. Greeting: After all make the sign of the cross, the president greets the assembled community with one of the following, adapted as necessary:

Gal. 1: 3
Col. 4: 18

or this greeting from *The Martyrdom of Polycarp:*

**Mercy, peace, and love to you
from God the Father and our Lord Jesus Christ.**

And also with you.

4. Opening prayer: The president may choose a suitable prayer from the sacramentary; or one may be composed, based on the theme developed in the readings chosen for this celebration. One example of this prayer:

**Let us pray to God our Father,
asking him to help us love others
as we wait in hope for our salvation.**

All pause for silent prayer.

**All praise to you, Father of all,
ruler of the universe:
you have loved us so fully
that you sent your Son to save us.**

**He loved us and gave his life for us,
dying so that we might die to sin,
rising so that we might wait in hope for your salvation.**

**Help us to work in faith and love
as we wait with hope
until he comes again in glory.**

**All glory and praise are yours, Father,
for ever and ever.**

Liturgy of the Word

God's word invites us to conversion and renewal of our life by proclaiming that Christ's death and rising have freed us from slavery to sin.

5. Readings from the word of God: The first reading is chosen from:

Titus 2: 11-14	lectionary, no. 14
1 Pet. 1: 3-9	no. 44

6. Meditative silence: A few moments of silence follow the reading, allowing all to reflect and pray in response to the word they have heard in faith.

7. Psalm: After silent prayer, a psalm or hymn is sung.

8. Second reading: If a second reading is used, it may be chosen from one of the New Testament texts above, or from readings in the seasonal lectionary. A moment of silent prayer follows this reading.

A gospel acclamation may be chosen from CBW II.

9. Gospel reading:

Mt. 25: 31-46	lectionary, no. 161
Mk. 13: 33-37	no. 2
Lk. 21: 25-28, 34-36	no. 3
Jn. 1: 6-8, 19-28	no. 8

10. Homily: The president proclaims the wonderful works and mercy of God as revealed in the scripture texts, and leads the assembly to prayer for sinners, to a reflective examination of conscience, and to repentance.

11. Prayer for sinners: The leader invites all to pray:

Let us pray for sinners
and ask God to forgive them:

All pause for silent prayer

Heavenly Father,
you do not want sinners to die,
but to live in grace and serve you in love.
Look upon the people of the world
and draw them back to you through Christ.

With him we pray:
Father, forgive them,
for they know not what they do!

Send your Spirit to soften hard hearts,
to bend rigid wills
and to warm those who are indifferent to you.

Father, forgive us our sins
and listen to our prayers for all sinners.
Bring them back to your love through our example,
so that with them we may praise you
and celebrate our thanks
through Christ our Lord.

12. Hymn: If desired, a hymn may be sung.

Examination of Christian Living

13. Examination of conscience: See pages 99-141.

14. Silent prayer: For about five minutes, all remain in silence. Sitting or kneeling as they wish, they discuss their way of life with the Lord.

15. Community act of sorrow:

Reader or president:
Lord, have you called us to be the people of love:
forgive us for choosing hatred and sin.
Lord, have mercy.

All: *Lord, have mercy.*

Christ, you have chosen us to do good,
to help others in your spirit of love:
forgive us for preferring to serve ourselves.
Christ, have mercy.

All: *Christ, have mercy.*

Lord, you have taught us to be the light of the world;
forgive us for choosing the kingdom of darkness.
Lord, have mercy.

All: *Lord, have mercy.*

16. Acclamation: A hymn may be sung.

Or a brief prayer of the faithful may be based on the theme, ending with the Lord's prayer (no. 17).

Conclusion of the Rite

17. Lord's Prayer: This prayer is best sung by all. The president may prepare an introduction to this prayer, based on the theme of the service. For example:

God has taught us to love one another
and to wait in hope for the coming of Jesus.
Let us pray together to our Father in love:

Our Father . . . .

18. Sacred action: The leader invites all to share the peace of Christ with one another, and introduces the rite in this way.

Jesus gives his forgiveness and peace
to all the people of God.
Let us share his peace and love with one another.

19. Invitation to the sacrament: The president may invite the congregation to celebrate the sacrament of penance after the bible service has ended.

20. Blessing: The leader may conclude with a simple blessing, or may use this form:

May the Father who has reconciled us in his love
continue to shower his blessing upon us.

All: *Amen!*

May the Son who died and rose to save us
forgive us our sins,
and help us to love one another more.

All: *Amen!*

May the Holy Spirit of God,
who makes us his temples of love and praise,
give us unending joy and peace.

All: *Amen!*

May our all-powerful God
— the Father, the + Son, and the Holy Spirit —
bless you and keep you for ever.

All: *Amen!*

21. Concluding hymn: All sing a seasonal hymn or song of praise.

SET FREE FROM WICKEDNESS

Entrance Rite

1. Song

2. Enthroning the word of God

3. Greeting: After all make the sign of the cross, the president greets the assembled community with one of the following, adapted as necessary:

> 1 Pet. 1: 2
> Gal. 1: 3

> or the following greeting from St. Clement of Rome:

> **All grace and peace to you**
> **from almighty God**
> **through Jesus Christ.**

> *And also with you.*

4. Opening prayer: The president may choose a suitable prayer from the sacramentary; or one may be composed, based on the theme developed in the readings chosen for this celebration. One example of this prayer:

> **Let us pray to God our Father,**
> **and praise him for sending his Son Jesus**
> **to set us free from wickedness.**

> All pause for silent prayer

> **Blessed are you, Father of all,**
> **ruler of the universe:**
> **you have loved us so fully**
> **that you sent your Son to save us.**
> **He loved us and gave his life for us,**
> **dying so that we might die to sin,**
> **rising in order to raise us to life in you.**

> **We praise you for saving us from sin**
> **and for making us your beloved people.**
> **Help us to love others**
> **as Jesus has loved us.**

> **All glory and praise are yours, Father,**
> **for ever and ever.**

Liturgy of the Word

God's word invites us to conversion and renewal of our life by proclaiming that Christ's death and rising have freed us from slavery to sin.

5. Readings from the word of God: The first reading may be chosen from:

Rom. 5: 12, 17-19	lectionary, no. 22
Eph. 5: 8-14	no. 31
Eph. 2: 4-10	no. 32
Rom. 8: 31-34	no. 26

6. Meditative silence: A few moments of silence should follow the reading, allowing all to reflect and pray in response to the word they have heard in faith.

7. Psalm: After silent prayer, a psalm or hymn is sung.

8. Second reading: If a second reading is used, it may be chosen from one of the New Testament texts above, or from readings in the seasonal lectionary. A moment of silent prayer follows this reading.

A gospel acclamation may be chosen from CBW II.

9. Gospel reading:

Lk. 13: 1-9	lectionary, no. 30
Jn. 3: 14-21	no. 32
Jn. 8: 1-11	no. 36
Mt. 6: 1-6, 16-18	no. 220

10. Homily: The president proclaims the wonderful works and mercy of God as revealed in the scripture texts, and leads the assembly to prayer for sinners, to a reflective examination of conscience, and to repentance.

11. Prayer for sinners: The leader invites all to pray:

**Let us pray for sinners
and ask God to forgive them:**

All pause for silent prayer

**Heavenly Father,
you do not want sinners to die,
but to live in grace and serve you in love.
Look upon the people of the world
and draw them back to you through Christ.**

**With him we pray:
Father, forgive them,
for they know not what they do!**

**Send your Spirit to soften hard hearts,
to bend rigid wills
and to warm those who are indifferent to you.**

**Father, forgive us our sins
and listen to our prayers for all sinners.
Bring them back to your love through our example,
so that with them we may praise you
and celebrate our thanks
through Christ our Lord.**

12. Hymn: If desired, a hymn may be sung.

Examination of Christian Living

13. Examination of conscience: See pages 99-141.

14. Silent prayer: For about five minutes, all remain in silence. Sitting or kneeling as they wish, they discuss their way of life with the Lord.

15. Community act of sorrow:

Reader or president:
**God has called us to be his people,
and has saved us through Jesus.
Let us pray to our Lord and ask his help.**

**Lord Jesus, you are the Son of God.
Lord, have mercy.**

All: *Lord, have mercy.*

**Christ, you are our Lord and savior.
Christ, have mercy.**

All: *Christ, have mercy.*

**Lord Jesus, we glorify your name.
Lord, have mercy.**

All: *Lord, have mercy.*

16. Acclamation: A hymn may be sung.

Or a brief prayer of the faithful may be based on the theme, ending with the Lord's prayer (no. 17).

Conclusion of the Rite

17. Lord's prayer: This prayer is best sung by all. The president may prepare an introduction to this prayer, based on the theme of the service. For example:

**God has given us his Son
to save us from our sins.
Let us pray with Jesus to our Father:**

Our Father . . . .

18. Sacred action: The leader invites all to share the peace of Christ with one another, and introduces the rite in this way.

**Jesus gives his forgiveness and peace
to all the people of God.
Let us share his peace and love with one another.**

19. Invitation to the sacrament: The president may invite the congregation to celebrate the sacrament of penance after the bible service has ended.

20. Blessing: The leader may conclude with a simple blessing, or may use this form:

**May God bless you with all good,
and protect you from all evil.**

All: *Amen!*

**May his life-giving wisdom enlighten your hearts,
and give you everlasting understanding.**

All: *Amen!*

**May he look upon you with mercy,
and raise you to unending happiness.**

All: *Amen!*

**May almighty God,
Father, Son, + and Holy Spirit,
give you his blessing for ever and ever.**

All: *Amen!*

21. Concluding hymn: All sing a seasonal hymn or song of praise.

LOVE OTHERS AS I LOVE YOU

Entrance Rite

1. Song

2. Enthroning the word of God

3. Greeting: After all make the sign of the cross, the president greets the assembled community with one of the following, adapted as necessary:

> Rom. 16: 29
> Phil. 4: 23

> or the following greeting from St. Ignatius of Antioch:

> **Every good wish to you**
> **for perfect joy in Jesus Christ.**
> *And also with you.*

4. Opening prayer: The president may choose a suitable prayer from the sacramentary; or one may be composed based on the theme developed in the readings chosen for this celebration. One example of this prayer:

> **Let us pray to God our Father,**
> **asking him to help us love others**
> **as Jesus has loved us.**

> All pause for silent prayer

> **Blessed are you, Father of all,**
> **ruler of the universe:**
> **you have loved us so fully**
> **that you sent your Son to save us.**

> **He loved us and gave his life for us,**
> **dying so that we might die to sin,**
> **rising in order to raise us to life in you.**

> **Help us to love others**
> **as Jesus has loved us.**

> **All glory and praise are yours, Father,**
> **for ever and ever.**

Liturgy of the Word

God's word invites us to conversion and renewal of our life by proclaiming that Christ's death and rising have freed us from slavery to sin.

5. Readings from the word of God

The first reading is chosen from:

Is. 48: 17-19	lectionary, no. 186
Rom. 13: 11-14	no. 1
1 Thess. 3: 12 — 4: 2	no. 3
Phil. 1: 4-6, 8-11	no. 6

6. Meditative silence: A few moments of silence should follow the reading, allowing all to reflect and pray in response to the word they have heard in faith.

7. Psalm: After silent prayer, a psalm or hymn is sung.

8. Second reading: If a second reading is used, it may be chosen from one of the New Testament texts above, or from seasonal readings in the lectionary. A moment of silent prayer follows this reading.

A gospel acclamation may be chosen from CBW II.

9. Gospel reading:

Jn. 13: 1-15	lectionary, no. 40
Jn. 13: 16-20	no. 282
Jn. 13: 31-33a, 34-35	no. 55
Jn. 14: 15-21	no. 56
Jn. 14: 23-29	no. 58
Jn. 15: 9-17	no. 57

10. Homily: The president proclaims the wonderful works and mercy of God as revealed in the scripture texts, and leads the assembly to prayer for sinners, to a reflective examination of conscience, and to repentance.

11. Prayer for sinners: The leader invites all to pray.

Let us pray for sinners
and ask God to forgive them:

All pause for silent prayer

Heavenly Father,
you do not want sinners to die,
but to live in grace and serve you in love.
Look upon the people of the world
and draw them back to you through Christ.
With him we pray:
Father, forgive them,
for they know not what they do!

Send your Spirit to soften hard hearts,
to bend rigid wills
and to warm those who are indifferent to you.

Father, forgive us our sins
and listen to our prayers for all sinners.
Bring them back to your love through our example,
so that with them we may praise you
and celebrate our thanks
through Christ our Lord.

12. Hymn: If desired, a hymn may be sung.

59

Examination of Christian Living

13. Examination of conscience: See pages 99-141.

14. Silent prayer: For about five minutes, all remain in silence. Sitting or kneeling as they wish, they discuss their way of life with the Lord.

15. Community act of sorrow:

Reader or president:
**Lord, you have called us to be the people of love:
forgive us for choosing hatred and sin.
Lord, have mercy.**

All: *Lord, have mercy.*

**Christ, you have chosen us to do good,
to help others in your spirit of love:
forgive us for preferring to serve ourselves.
Christ, have mercy.**

All: *Christ, have mercy.*

**Lord, you have taught us to be the light of the world;
forgive us for failing to be people of light.
Lord, have mercy.**

All: *Lord, have mercy.*

16. Acclamation: A hymn may be sung.

Or a brief prayer of the faithful may be based on the theme, ending with the Lord's prayer (no. 17).

Conclusion of the Rite

17. Lord's Prayer: This prayer is best sung by all. The president may prepare an introduction to this prayer, based on the theme of the service. For example:

**God has taught us to love one another
as Jesus has loved us.
Let us pray together to our Father in love:**

Our Father . . . .

18. Sacred action: The leader invites all to share the peace of Christ with one another, and introduces the rite in this way:

**Jesus gives his forgiveness and peace
to all the people of God.
Let us share his peace and love with one another.**

19. Invitation to the sacrament: The leader may conclude with a simple blessing, or may use this form:

**May the Father who has reconciled us in his love
continue to shower his blessings upon us.**

All: *Amen!*

**May the Son who died and rose to save us
forgive us our sins,
and help us to love one another more.**

All: *Amen!*

**May the Holy Spirit of God,
who makes us his temples of love and praise,
give us unending joy and peace.**

All: *Amen!*

**May you be protected and blessed,
and made strong in faith, hope, and love
by our all-powerful and loving God,
the Father, the + Son, and the Holy Spirit.**

All: *Amen!*

21. Concluding hymn: All sing a seasonal hymn or song of praise.

DYING TO SIN, LIVING FOR GOD

Entrance Rite

1. Song

2. Enthroning the word of God

3. Greeting: After all make the sign of the cross, the president greets the assembled community with one of the following, adapted as necessary:

Eph. 6: 24
1 Cor. 16: 23

or the following greeting from St. Polycarp:

May mercy and peace be yours
from almighty God and Jesus Christ our savior.

And also with you.

4. Opening prayer: The president may choose a suitable prayer from the sacramentary; or one may be composed, based on the theme developed in the readings chosen for this celebration. One example of this prayer:

Let us pray to God our Father,
asking him to help us die to sin,
and to live the life of grace.

All pause for silent prayer.

Blessed are you, Father of all,
ruler of the universe:
you have loved us so fully
that you sent your Son to save us.

In obedience to your will
he accepted death on the cross,
and you raised him in glory to give us new life.
Help us to die to sin and live for God.
Open our hearts to listen to your Spirit,
and make us eager to live the life of grace.

All glory and praise are yours, Father,
for ever and ever.

Liturgy of the Word

God's word invites us to conversion and renewal of our life by proclaiming that Christ's death and rising have freed us from slavery to sin, and have made us his people of praise.

5. Reading from the word of God: The first reading may be chosen from:

Rom. 6: 3-11	lectionary, no. 42
Col. 1: 12-20	no. 163
Heb. 9: 24-28	no. 156
Heb. 4: 14-16	no. 147

6. Meditative silence: A few moments of silence follow the reading, allowing all to reflect and pray in response to the word they have heard in faith.

7. Psalm: After silent prayer, a psalm or hymn is sung.

8. Second reading: If a second reading is used, it may be chosen from one of the New Testament texts above, or from readings in the seasonal lectionary. A moment of silent prayer follows this reading.

A gospel acclamation may be chosen from CBW II.

9. Gospel reading:

Lk. 18: 9-14	lectionary, no. 151
Lk. 23: 35-43	no. 163
Jn. 8: 31-36	no. 254
Jn. 15: 9-17	no. 57

10. Homily: The president proclaims the wonderful works and mercy of God as revealed in the scripture texts, and leads the assembly to prayer for sinners, to a reflective examination of conscience, and to repentance.

11. Prayer for sinners: The leader invites all to pray:

**Let us pray for sinners
and ask God to forgive them:**

All pause for silent prayer.

**Heavenly Father,
you do not want sinners to die,
but to live in grace and serve you in love.
Look upon the people of the world
and draw them back to you through Christ.**

**With him we pray:
Father, forgive them, for they know not what they do!**

**Send your Spirit to soften hard hearts,
to bend rigid wills,
to warm those who are indifferent to you,
and to lead them to give you praise.**

**Father,
forgive us our sins
and listen to our prayers for all sinners.
Bring them back to your love through our example,
so that with them we may praise you
and celebrate our thanks through Christ our Lord.**

12. Hymn: If desired, a hymn may be sung.

Examination of Christian Living

13. Examination of conscience: See pages 99-141.

14. Silent prayer: For about five minutes, all remain in silence. Sitting or kneeling as they wish, they discuss their way of life with the Lord.

15. Community act of sorrow:

Reader or president:
Lord, you have taught us to be the light of the world:
forgive us for failing to be people of light.
Lord, have mercy.

All: *Lord, have mercy.*

Christ, you have called us to be the people of love:
forgive us for choosing hatred and sin.
Christ, have mercy.

All: *Christ, have mercy.*

Lord, you have chosen us to do good,
to serve others in your Spirit of love:
forgive us for preferring to serve ourselves.
Lord, have mercy.

All: *Lord, have mercy.*

16. Acclamation: A hymn may be sung.

Or a brief form of the general intercessions may be based on the theme, ending with the Lord's prayer (no. 17).

Conclusion of the Rite

17. Lord's prayer: This prayer is best sung by all. The president may prepare an introduction to this prayer, based on the theme of the service. For example:

Jesus has invited us to live as the children of God.
Let us join our savior as we pray:

Our Father . . . .

18. Sacred action: The leader invites all to share the peace of Christ with one another, and introduces the rite in this way:

Jesus gives his forgiveness and peace
to all the people of God.
Let us share his peace and love with one another.

19. Invitation to the sacrament: The president may invite the congregation to celebrate the sacrament of penance after the bible service has ended.

20. Blessing: The leader may conclude with a simple blessing, or may use this form:

**May the Father of light bless you with all good,
and protect you from all evil.**

All: *Amen!*

**May his wisdom enlighten your hearts,
and give you everlasting understanding.**

All: *Amen!*

**May he look upon you with mercy,
and raise you to unending happiness.**

All: *Amen!*

**May our all-powerful God
— the Father, the + Son, and the Holy Spirit —
bless you and keep you for ever.**

All: *Amen!*

21. Concluding hymn: All sing a seasonal hymn or song of praise.

RECONCILIATION WITH OTHERS

Entrance Rite

1. Song

2. Enthroning the word of God

3. Greeting: After all make the sign of the cross, the president greets the assembled community with one of the following, adapted as necessary:

> 2 Cor. 1: 2
> Rom. 1: 7b

> or the following greeting from St. Polycarp:

> **May mercy and peace be with you
> from almighty God and Jesus Christ our savior.**

> *And also with you.*

4. Opening prayer: The president may choose a suitable prayer from the sacramentary; or one may be composed, based on the theme developed in the readings chosen for this celebration. One example of this prayer:

> **Let us pray to God our Father,
> asking him to reconcile us with all people,
> for Jesus died that everyone might be saved:**

> All pause for silent prayer.

> **Praise to you, Lord God, king of the universe:
> you have chosen us to be your beloved children,
> united to you in your Son, our savior.**

> **Lead us from sin
> and help us to love and forgive others
> as you have loved and forgiven us.**

> **Father,
> we praise you and bless your name
> through Jesus Christ our Lord.**

Liturgy of the Word

God's word invites us to conversion and renewal of our life by proclaiming that Christ's death and rising have freed us from slavery to sin, and have made us his people of praise.

5. Reading from the word of God: The first reading may be chosen from:

Sir. 27: 33 — 28: 9	lectionary, no. 131
2 Cor. 5: 20 — 6: 2	no. 220
Col. 1: 12-20	no. 163

6. Meditative silence: A few moments of silence follow the reading, allowing all to reflect and pray in response to the word they have heard in faith.

7. Psalm: After silent prayer, a psalm or hymn is sung.

8. Second reading: If a second reading is used, it may be chosen from one of the New Testament texts above, or from readings in the seasonal lectionary. A moment of silent prayer follows this reading.

A gospel acclamation may be chosen from CBW II.

9. Gospel reading:

Mt. 5: 20-26	lectionary, no. 229
Mt. 18: 21-35	no. 131
Lk. 7: 36-50	no. 446

10. Homily: The president proclaims the wonderful works and mercy of God as revealed in the scripture texts, and leads the assembly to prayer for sinners, to a reflective examination of conscience, and to repentance.

11. Prayer for sinners: The leader invites all to pray:

Let us pray for sinners
and ask God to forgive them:

All pause for silent prayer.

Heavenly Father,
you do not want sinners to die,
but to live in grace and serve you in love.
Look upon the people of the world
and draw them back to you through Christ.

With him we pray:
Father, forgive them, for they know not what they do!

Send your Spirit to soften hard hearts,
to bend rigid wills,
to warm those who are indifferent to you,
and to lead them to give you praise.

Father,
forgive us our sins
and listen to our prayers for all sinners.
Bring them back to your love through our example,
so that with them we may praise you
and celebrate our thanks through Christ our Lord.

12. Hymn: If desired, a hymn may be sung.

Examination of Christian Living

13. Examination of conscience: See pages 99-141.

14. Silent prayer: For about five minutes, all remain in silence. Sitting or kneeling as they wish, they discuss their way of life with the Lord.

15. Community act of sorrow:

Reader or president:
**Lord, you have called us to be the children of light:
forgive us for choosing the darkness of sin.
Lord, have mercy.**

All: *Lord, have mercy.*

**Christ, you have chosen us to do good
and help others in your spirit of love:
forgive us for preferring to serve ourselves.
Christ, have mercy.**

All: *Christ, have mercy.*

**Lord, you have taught us to be the light of the world;
forgive us for bringing darkness into the lives of others.
Lord, have mercy.**

All: *Lord, have mercy.*

16. Acclamation: A hymn may be sung.

Or a brief form of the general intercessions may be based on the theme, ending with the Lord's prayer (no. 17).

Conclusion of the Rite

17. Lord's prayer: This prayer is best sung by all. The president may prepare an introduction to this prayer, based on the theme of the service. For example:

**God has reconciled us
to himself and to one another
by the death and resurrection of his Son.
Let us pray to our Father in love:**

Our Father . . . .

18. Sacred action: The leader invites all to share the peace of Christ with one another, and introduces the rite in this way:

**Jesus gives his forgiveness and peace
to all the people of God.
Let us share his peace and love with one another.**

19. Invitation to the sacrament: The president may invite the congregation to celebrate the sacrament of penance after the bible service has ended.

20. Blessing: The leader may conclude with a simple blessing, or may use this form:

**May the Father who has reconciled us in his love
continue to shower his blessings upon us.**

All: *Amen!*

**May the Son who died and rose to save us
forgive us our sins
and lead us in his footsteps.**

All: *Amen!*

**May the Holy Spirit of God,
who makes us his temples of love and praise,
give us unending joy and peace.**

All: *Amen!*

**May almighty God,
Father, Son, + and Holy Spirit,
give you his blessing for ever and ever.**

All: *Amen!*

21. Concluding hymn: All sing a seasonal hymn or song of praise.

RECONCILIATION WITH GOD

Entrance Rite

1. Song

2. Enthroning the word of God

3. Greeting: After all make the sign of the cross, the president greets the assembled community with one of the following, adapted as necessary:

Eph. 1: 2
Phil. 1: 2

or the following greeting from St. Ignatius of Antioch:

**All happiness to you
in God the Father and in Jesus Christ.**

And also with you.

4. Opening prayer: The president may choose a suitable prayer from the sacramentary; or one may be composed, based on the theme developed in the readings chosen for this celebration. One example of this prayer:

**Let us pray to our Father in heaven,
and ask him to reconcile us and all his people:**

All pause for silent prayer.

**Blessed are you, Lord God, king of all creation:
you have made us your beloved people.**

**Open our hearts to your loving mercy.
Help us to turn away from sin
and thus come back to your loving service.**

**Father, we give you praise and glory
through Jesus Christ your Son.**

Liturgy of the Word

God's word invites us to conversion and renewal of our life by proclaiming that Christ's death and rising have freed us from slavery to sin, and have made us his people of praise.

5. Reading from the word of God: The first reading may be chosen from:

Eph. 2: 4-10	lectionary, no. 32
1 Tim. 1: 12-17	no. 133

6. Meditative silence: A few moments of silence follow the reading, allowing all to reflect and pray in response to the word they have heard in faith.

7. Psalm: After silent prayer, a psalm or hymn is sung.

8. Second reading: If a second reading is used, it may be chosen from one of the New Testament texts above, or from readings in the seasonal lectionary. A moment of silent prayer follows this reading.

A gospel acclamation may be chosen from CBW II.

9. Gospel reading:

Jn. 6: 60-69	lectionary, no. 123
Jn. 8: 21-30	no. 253
Lk. 15: 1-3, 11-32	no. 33

10. Homily: The president proclaims the wonderful works and mercy of God as revealed in the scripture texts, and leads the assembly to prayer for sinners, to a reflective examination of conscience, and to repentance.

11. Prayer for sinners: The leader invites all to pray:

**Let us pray for sinners
and ask God to forgive them:**

All pause for silent prayer.

**Heavenly Father,
you do not want sinners to die,
but to live in grace and serve you in love.
Look upon the people of the world
and draw them back to you through Christ.**

**With him we pray:
Father, forgive them, for they know not what they do!**

**Send your Spirit to soften hard hearts,
to bend rigid wills,
to warm those who are indifferent to you,
and to lead them to give you praise.**

**Father,
forgive us our sins
and listen to our prayers for all sinners.
Bring them back to your love through our example,
so that with them we may praise you
and celebrate our thanks through Christ our Lord.**

12. Hymn: If desired, a hymn may be sung.

Examination of Christian Living

13. Examination of conscience: See pages 99-141.

14. Silent prayer: For about five minutes, all remain in silence. Sitting or kneeling as they wish, they discuss their way of life with the Lord.

15. Community act of sorrow:

Reader or president:
**God has called us to be his people,
and has saved us through Jesus.
Let us pray to our Lord and ask his help.**

**Lord Jesus, you are the light of the world:
Lord, have mercy.**

All: *Lord, have mercy.*

**You are our savior and the Lord of glory:
Christ, have mercy.**

All: *Christ, have mercy.*

**You are the bread of life:
Lord, have mercy.**

All: *Lord, have mercy.*

16. Acclamation: A hymn may be sung.

Or a brief form of the general intercessions may be based on the theme, ending with the Lord's prayer (no. 17).

Conclusion of the Rite

17. Lord's prayer: This prayer is best sung by all. The president may prepare an introduction to this prayer, based on the theme of the service. For example:

**God has reconciled us to himself
through the death and resurrection of his Son.
Let us pray to him in union with the Lord Jesus:**

Our Father . . . .

18. Sacred action: The leader invites all to share the peace of Christ with one another, and introduces the rite in this way:

**Jesus gives God's forgiveness and peace
to all who believe and repent.
Let us share his peace and love with one another.**

19. Invitation to the sacrament: The president may invite the congregation to celebrate the sacrament of penance after the bible service has ended.

20. Blessing: The leader may conclude with a simple blessing, or may use this form:

**May the Father who has reconciled us in his love
continue to shower his blessings upon us.**

All: *Amen!*

May the Son who died and rose to save us
forgive us our sins
and lead us in his footsteps.

All: *Amen!*

May the Holy Spirit of God,
who makes us his temples of love and praise,
give us unending joy and peace.

All: *Amen!*

May you be protected and blessed,
and made strong in faith, hope, and love
by our all-powerful and loving God,
the Father, the + Son, and the Holy Spirit.

All: *Amen!*

21. Concluding hymn: All sing a seasonal hymn or song of praise.

GOD'S CHOSEN PEOPLE

Entrance Rite

1. Song

2. Enthroning the word of God

3. Greeting: After all make the sign of the cross, the president greets the assembled community with one of the following, adapted as necessary:

> 1 Tim. 1: 2
> Rev. 1: 4-6
> Jude 1-2

4. Opening prayer: The president may choose a suitable prayer from the sacramentary; or one may be composed, based on the theme developed in the readings chosen for this celebration. One example of this prayer:

> **Let us pray for the grace**
> **to live as God's holy people,**
> **chosen to do his work on earth:**

> All pause for silent prayer

> **Loving Father,**
> **listen to the prayers of your people.**
> **We praise you for having chosen us in Jesus**
> **to sing your praises by our words and works:**
> **help us to live lives worthy of our Christian vocation.**

> **We ask this grace**
> **in the name of Jesus the Lord.**

Liturgy of the Word

God's word invites us to conversion and renewal of our life by proclaiming that Christ's death and rising have freed us from slavery to sin, and have made us his people of praise.

5. Reading from the word of God: The first reading may be chosen from:

Eph. 1: 3-14	lectionary, no. 105
Col. 1: 9-14	no. 434
Titus 2: 11-14	no. 14
Col. 3: 12-17	no. 440

6. Meditative silence: A few moments of silence follow the reading, allowing all to reflect and pray in response to the word they have heard in faith.

7. Psalm: After silent prayer, a psalm or hymn is sung.

8. Second reading: If a second reading is used, it may be chosen from one of the New Testament texts above, or from readings in the seasonal lectionary. A moment of silent prayer follows this reading.

A gospel acclamation may be chosen from CBW II.

9. Gospel reading:

Mt. 5: 13-16	lectionary, no. 74
Mt. 5: 1-12	no. 71
Jn. 15: 1-9	no. 54

10. Homily: The president proclaims the wonderful works and mercy of God as revealed in the scripture texts, and leads the assembly to prayer for sinners, to a reflective examination of conscience, and to repentance.

11. Prayer for sinners: The leader invites all to pray:

**Let us pray for sinners
and ask God to forgive them:**

All pause for silent prayer.

**Heavenly Father,
you do not want sinners to die,
but to live in grace and serve you in love.
Look upon the people of the world
and draw them back to you through Christ.**

**With him we pray:
Father, forgive them, for they know not what they do!**

**Send your Spirit to soften hard hearts,
to bend rigid wills,
to warm those who are indifferent to you,
and to lead them to give you praise.**

**Father,
forgive us our sins
and listen to our prayers for all sinners.
Bring them back to your love through our example,
so that with them we may praise you
and celebrate our thanks through Christ our Lord.**

12. Hymn: If desired, a hymn may be sung.

Examination of Christian Living

13. Examination of conscience: See pages 99-141.

14. Silent prayer: For about five minutes, all remain in silence. Sitting or kneeling as they wish, they discuss their way of life with the Lord.

15. Community act of sorrow:

Lord, you have called us to be the children of light:
forgive us for choosing the darkness of sin.
Lord, have mercy.

All: *Lord, have mercy.*

Christ, you have chosen us to do good
and help others in your spirit of love:
forgive us for preferring to serve ourselves.
Christ, have mercy.

All: *Christ, have mercy.*

Lord, you have taught us to be the light of the world;
forgive us for bringing darkness into the lives of others.
Lord, have mercy.

All: *Lord, have mercy.*

16. Acclamation: A hymn may be sung.

Or a brief form of the general intercessions may be based on the theme, ending with the Lord's prayer (no. 17).

Conclusion of the Rite

17. Lord's prayer: This prayer is best sung by all. The president may prepare an introduction to this prayer, based on the theme of the service. For example:

Lord Jesus,
remember us in your kingdom
and teach us to join you in saying:

Our Father . . . .

18. Sacred action: The leader invites all to share the peace of Christ with one another, and introduces the rite in this way:

Jesus gives his forgiveness and peace
to all the people of God.
Let us share his peace and love with one another.

19. Invitation to the sacrament: The president may invite the congregation to celebrate the sacrament of penance after the bible service has ended.

20. Blessing: The leader may conclude with a simple blessing, or may use this form:

May the Father who has called us to be his people
continue to shower his blessings upon us.

All: *Amen!*

**May the Son who died and rose to save us
forgive us our sins
and lead us in his footsteps.**

All: *Amen!*

**May the Holy Spirit of God,
who makes us his temples of love and praise,
give us unending joy and peace.**

All: *Amen!*

**May almighty God,
Father, Son, + and Holy Spirit,
give you his blessing for ever and ever.**

All: *Amen!*

21. Concluding hymn: All sing a seasonal hymn or song of praise.

PREPARE THE WAY OF THE LORD

Entrance Rite

1. Song

2. Enthroning the word of God

3. Greeting: After all make the sign of the cross, the president greets the assembled community with one of the following, adapted as necessary:

> 1 Peter 1: 2b
> Jude v. 25

> **May the God of hope**
> **bring you such joy and peace in your faith**
> **that the power of the Holy Spirit**
> **will remove all bounds to hope.**

> *Blessed be God, the Father of our Lord Jesus Christ.*

4. Opening prayer: The president may choose a suitable prayer from the sacramentary; or one may be composed, based on the theme developed in the readings chosen for this celebration. One example of this prayer:

> **Let us pray to God our Father,**
> **and praise him for sending his Son**
> **to bring new life to all who believe.**

> All pause for silent prayer.

> **All praise and glory to you, Father,**
> **creator and ruler of the universe:**
> **You sent your Son to be one with us**
> **and call us to the fullness of grace and life.**

> **Open our hearts to your love.**
> **Help us to overcome sin,**
> **and give you praise by serving others.**
> **Fill us with mercy and compassion to all.**

> **All praise and glory are yours, Father,**
> **for ever and ever.**

Liturgy of the Word

God's word invites us to conversion and renewal of our life by proclaiming that Christ's death and rising have freed us from slavery to sin, and have made us his people of praise.

5. Reading from the word of God: The first reading may be chosen from:

Ezek. 36: 25-27, 28b	lectionary, no. 42
Col. 2: 6-8	438
James 1: 19-27	337
1 Pet. 1: 13-16	348

6. Meditative silence: A few moments of silence follow the reading, allowing all to reflect and pray in response to the word they have heard in faith.

7. Psalm: After silent prayer, a psalm or hymn is sung.

8. Second reading: If a second reading is used, it may be chosen from one of the New Testament texts above, or from readings in the seasonal lectionary. A moment of silent prayer follows this reading.

A gospel acclamation may be chosen from CBW II.

9. Gospel reading:

Mt. 3: 1-12	lectionary, no. 4
Mk. 1: 2-8	5
Lk. 3: 2-18	—
Jn. 1: 19-28	8

10. Homily: The president proclaims the wonderful works and mercy of God as revealed in the scripture texts, and leads the assembly to prayer for sinners, to a reflective examination of conscience, and to repentance.

11. Prayer for sinners: The leader invites all to pray:

**Let us pray for sinners
and ask God to forgive them:**

All pause for silent prayer.

**Heavenly Father,
you do not want sinners to die,
but to live in grace and serve you in love.
Look upon the people of the world
and draw them back to you through Christ.**

**With him we pray:
Father, forgive them, for they know not what they do!**

**Send your Spirit to soften hard hearts,
to bend rigid wills,
to warm those who are indifferent to you,
and to lead them to give you praise.**

**Father,
forgive us our sins
and listen to our prayers for all sinners.
Bring them back to your love through our example,
so that with them we may praise you
and celebrate our thanks through Christ our Lord.**

12. Hymn: If desired, a hymn may be sung.

Examination of Christian Living

13. Examination of conscience: See pages 99-141.

14. Silent prayer: For about five minutes, all remain in silence. Sitting or kneeling as they wish, they discuss their way of life with the Lord.

15. Community act of sorrow:

Lord Jesus, light in our darkness:
Lord, have mercy.

All: *Lord, have mercy.*

Christ, strength in our weakness:
Christ, have mercy.

All: *Christ, have mercy.*

Lord Jesus, helper in our time of need:
Lord, have mercy.

All: *Lord, have mercy.*

The leader concludes with these or similar words:

The Lord Jesus died to save all sinners
and was raised to bring us the life of grace.
May he forgive us our sins
and let us share in his glory for ever.

All: *Amen!*

16. Acclamation: A hymn may be sung.

Or a brief form of the general intercessions may be based on the theme, ending with the Lord's prayer (no. 17).

Conclusion of the Rite

17. Lord's prayer: This prayer is best sung by all. The president may prepare an introduction to this prayer, based on the theme of the service. For example:

God has called us to be his people of praise.
Let us pray with Jesus to our Father:

Our Father . . .

18. Sacred action: The leader invites all to share the peace of Christ with one another, and introduces the rite in this way:

Jesus gives his forgiveness and peace
to all the people of God.
Let us share his peace and love with one another.

19. Invitation to the sacrament: The president may invite the congregation to celebrate the sacrament of penance after the bible service has ended.

20. Blessing: The leader may conclude with a simple blessing, or may use this form:

**The Father, Son, and Spirit live
in the hearts of those who love God and neighbor.
May God remain with us
and guide us in our works of love.**

All: *Amen!*

**May our all-powerful God
— the Father, the + Son, and the Holy Spirit —
bless us and keep us for ever.**

All: *Amen!*

21. Concluding hymn: All sing a seasonal hymn or song of praise.

FORGIVE OTHERS AS I FORGIVE YOU

Entrance Rite

1. Song

2. Enthroning the word of God

3. Greeting: After all make the sign of the cross, the president greets the assembled community with one of the following, adapted as necessary:

> 1 Thess. 1: 1
> Heb. 13: 20-21
> 2 Pet. 1: 1-2

or the following greeting from St. Ignatius of Antioch:

**All happiness to you
in God the Father and in Jesus Christ.**

And also with you.

4. Opening prayer: The president may choose a suitable prayer from the sacramentary; or one may be composed, based on the theme developed in the readings chosen for this celebration. One example of this prayer:

**Let us pray for the grace to forgive others
as generously as God has forgiven us:**

All pause for silent prayer.

**Lord Jesus,
listen to our prayer
and bring it to our heavenly Father.
In your mercy and love,
teach us to love and forgive others
as you have loved and forgiven us.
Have mercy on your people
and lead us to the joys of heaven,
where you are Lord for ever and ever.**

Liturgy of the Word

God's word invites us to conversion and renewal of our life by proclaiming that Christ's death and rising have freed us from slavery to sin, and have made us his people of praise.

5. Reading from the word of God: The first reading may be chosen from:

> Sirach 28: 1-7 —
> Ezek. 36: 20-32 —
> Eph. 5: 1-14 —
> 1 Jn. 3: 1-24 —

6. Meditative silence: A few moments of silence follow the reading, allowing all to reflect and pray in response to the word they have heard in faith.

7. Psalm: After silent prayer, a psalm or hymn is sung.

8. Second reading: If a second reading is used, it may be chosen from one of the New Testament texts above, or from readings in the seasonal lectionary. A moment of silent prayer follows this reading.

A gospel acclamation may be chosen from CBW II.

9. Gospel reading:

Mt. 18: 21-35	lectionary, no. 131
Mk. 12: 28-34	153
Lk. 17: 1-6	—
Jn. 19: 13-37	—

10. Homily: The president proclaims the wonderful works and mercy of God as revealed in the scripture texts, and leads the assembly to prayer for sinners, to a reflective examination of conscience, and to repentance.

11. Prayer for sinners: The leader invites all to pray:

**Let us pray for sinners
and ask God to forgive them:**

All pause for silent prayer.

**Heavenly Father,
you do not want sinners to die,
but to live in grace and serve you in love.
Look upon the people of the world
and draw them back to you through Christ.**

**With him we pray:
Father, forgive them, for they know not what they do!**

**Send your Spirit to soften hard hearts,
to bend rigid wills,
to warm those who are indifferent to you,
and to lead them to give you praise.**

**Father,
forgive us our sins
and listen to our prayers for all sinners.
Bring them back to your love through our example,
so that with them we may praise you
and celebrate our thanks through Christ our Lord.**

12. Hymn: If desired, a hymn may be sung.

Examination of Christian Living

13. Examination of conscience: See pages 99-141.

14. Silent prayer: For about five minutes, all remain in silence. Sitting or kneeling as they wish, they discuss their way of life with the Lord.

15. Community act of sorrow:

Good shepherd of all and Lamb of God:
Lord, have mercy.

All: *Lord, have mercy.*

Living vine and bread of life:
Christ, have mercy.

All: *Christ, have mercy.*

Word of God, sent to save us all:
Lord, have mercy.

All: *Lord, have mercy.*

16. Acclamation: A hymn may be sung.

Or a brief form of the general intercessions may be based on the theme, ending with the Lord's prayer (no. 17).

Conclusion of the Rite

17. Lord's prayer: This prayer is best sung by all. The president may prepare an introduction to this prayer, based on the theme of the service. For example:

Let us pray to our heavenly Father,
asking his forgiveness and love:

Our Father . . .

18. Sacred action: The leader invites all to share the peace of Christ with one another, and introduces the rite in this way:

Jesus gives his forgiveness and peace
to all the people of God.
Let us share his peace and love with one another.

19. Invitation to the sacrament: The president may invite the congregation to celebrate the sacrament of penance after the bible service has ended.

20. Blessing: The leader may conclude with a simple blessing, or may use this form:

May the Father of forgiveness bless you
and bring you to everlasting life.

All: *Amen!*

**May the Son who died and rose to save us
forgive us our sins
and lead us in his footsteps.**

All: *Amen!*

**May the Holy Spirit of God
pour out his love upon you
and fill you with joy and peace.**

All: *Amen!*

**May you be protected and blessed,
and made strong in faith, hope, and love
by our all-powerful and loving God,
the Father, the + Son, and the Holy Spirit.**

All: *Amen!*

21. Concluding hymn: All sing a seasonal hymn or song of praise.

THE PEACE OF CHRIST

Entrance Rite

1. Song

2. Enthroning the word of God

3. Greeting: After all make the sign of the cross, the president greets the assembled community with one of the following, adapted as necessary:

> Eph. 1: 2
> 2 Tim. 1: 2
> 2 Thess. 1: 2

4. Opening prayer: The president may choose a suitable prayer from the sacramentary; or one may be composed, based on the theme developed in the readings chosen for this celebration. One example of this prayer:

> **We bow our heads in prayer,**
> **and pray to God for peace.**
>
> All pause for a moment of silent prayer.
>
> **Father of our Lord Jesus Christ,**
> **have mercy on all the world.**
> **Pour the Spirit of peace into the hearts of all,**
> **and help us to be peacemakers**
> **who work for harmony and love.**
>
> **Grant us this gift**
> **through Jesus our Lord.**
>
> All: *Amen!*

Liturgy of the Word

God's word invites us to conversion and renewal of our life by proclaiming that Christ's death and rising have freed us from slavery to sin, and have made us his people of praise.

5. Reading from the word of God: The first reading may be chosen from:

> Is. 9: 1-6   lectionary, no. 831(1)
> Is. 32: 15-18   831(2)
> Phil. 4: 6-9   832(1)
> James 3: 13-18   832(2)

6. Meditative silence: A few moments of silence follow the reading, allowing all to reflect and pray in response to the word they have heard in faith.

7. Psalm: After silent prayer, a psalm or hymn is sung.

8. Second reading: If a second reading is used, it may be chosen from one of the New Testament texts above, or from readings in the seasonal lectionary. A moment of silent prayer follows this reading.

A gospel acclamation may be chosen from CBW II.

9. Gospel reading:

Mt. 5: 1-12a	lectionary, no. 71
Jn. 20: 19-23	835(4)
Jn. 14: 23-29	116

10. Homily: The president proclaims the wonderful works and mercy of God as revealed in the scripture texts, and leads the assembly to prayer for sinners, to a reflective examination of conscience, and to repentance.

11. Prayer for sinners: The leader invites all to pray:

**Let us pray for sinners
and ask God to forgive them:**

All pause for silent prayer.

**Heavenly Father,
you do not want sinners to die,
but to live in grace and serve you in love.
Look upon the people of the world
and draw them back to you through Christ.**

**With him we pray:
Father, forgive them, for they know not what they do!**

**Send your Spirit to soften hard hearts,
to bend rigid wills,
to warm those who are indifferent to you,
and to lead them to give you praise.**

**Father,
forgive us our sins
and listen to our prayers for all sinners.
Bring them back to your love through our example,
so that with them we may praise you
and celebrate our thanks through Christ our Lord.**

12. Hymn: If desired, a hymn may be sung.

Examination of Christian Living

13. Examination of conscience: See pages 99-141.

14. Silent prayer: For about five minutes, all remain in silence. Sitting or kneeling as they wish, they discuss their way of life with the Lord.

15. Community act of sorrow:

Reader or president:
**People of God,
let us remember that we are called to be holy,
and ask the Lord Jesus to forgive us our sins.**

All pause for a moment of silent prayer.

**Savior of the world, you died to save us from sin:
Lord, have mercy.**

All: *Lord, have mercy.*

**Hope of sinners, you have been raised to give us new life:
Christ, have mercy.**

All: *Christ, have mercy.*

**Son of God, you are with the Father in glory:
Lord, have mercy.**

All: *Lord, have mercy.*

16. Acclamation: A hymn may be sung.

Or a brief form of the general intercessions may be based on the theme, ending with the Lord's prayer (no. 17).

Conclusion of the Rite

17. Lord's prayer: This prayer is best sung by all. The president may prepare an introduction to this prayer, based on the theme of the service. For example:

**God has called us to be his people of peace.
Let us pray to our Father in peace.**

Our Father . . .

18. Sacred action: The leader invites all to share the peace of Christ with one another, and introduces the rite in this way:

**Jesus gives his forgiveness and peace
to all the people of God.
Let us share his peace and love with one another.**

19. Invitation to the sacrament: The president may invite the congregation to celebrate the sacrament of penance after the bible service has ended.

20. Blessing: The leader may conclude with a simple blessing, or may use this form:

May God our Father bless us in all our prayers.

All: *Amen!*

**May God the Son, Jesus Christ our Lord,
strengthen us in his love.**

All: *Amen!*

**May God the Holy Spirit
guide us in all our deeds.**

All: *Amen!*

**May our all-powerful God
— the Father, the + Son, and the Holy Spirit —
bless us and keep us for ever.**

All: *Amen!*

21. Concluding hymn: All sing a seasonal hymn or song of praise.

CHRIST IS THE LIGHT OF THE WORLD

Entrance Rite

1. Song

2. Enthroning the word of God

3. Greeting: After all make the sign of the cross, the president greets the assembled community with one of the following, adapted as necessary:

> 2 Tim. 1: 2
> Titus 1: 4
> 1 Pet. 5: 14

or the following greeting from St. Ignatius of Antioch:

**Greetings in the blood of Christ
where we find unfailing and eternal joy.**

And also with you.

4. Opening prayer: The president may choose a suitable prayer from the sacramentary; or one may be composed, based on the theme developed in the readings chosen for this celebration. One example of this prayer:

**Let us pray to our Father in heaven,
who sent his Son to be the light of the world:**

All pause for silent prayer.

**Loving Father,
we praise you for having chosen us
to be your holy people,
your instruments for saving the world.**

**Grant that we may once more cast sin out of our lives
so that we may truly be the children of light.
Father, we ask this grace through Christ our Lord.**

Liturgy of the Word

God's word invites us to conversion and renewal of our life by proclaiming that Christ's death and rising have freed us from slavery to sin, and have made us his people of praise.

5. Reading from the word of God: The first reading may be chosen from:

	lectionary, no.
Mic. 7: 7-9	244
Col. 1: 11-20	163
1 Jn. 1: 5-10	698
1 Jn. 2: 7-11	203
1 Jn. 3: 1-10	—

6. Meditative silence: A few moments of silence follow the reading, allowing all to reflect and pray in response to the word they have heard in faith.

7. Psalm: After silent prayer, a psalm or hymn is sung.

8. Second reading: If a second reading is used, it may be chosen from one of the New Testament texts above, or from readings in the seasonal lectionary. A moment of silent prayer follows this reading.

A gospel acclamation may be chosen from CBW II.

9. Gospel reading:

Mt. 5: 13-16	lectionary, no. 74
Jn. 1: 1-18	16
Jn. 12: 31-36a	902(4)
Lk. 11: 33-36	—

10. Homily: The president proclaims the wonderful works and mercy of God as revealed in the scripture texts, and leads the assembly to prayer for sinners, to a reflective examination of conscience, and to repentance.

11. Prayer for sinners: The leader invites all to pray:

**Let us pray for sinners
and ask God to forgive them:**

All pause for silent prayer.

**Heavenly Father,
you do not want sinners to die,
but to live in grace and serve you in love.
Look upon the people of the world
and draw them back to you through Christ.**

**With him we pray:
Father, forgive them, for they know not what they do!**

**Send your Spirit to soften hard hearts,
to bend rigid wills,
to warm those who are indifferent to you,
and to lead them to give you praise.**

**Father,
forgive us our sins
and listen to our prayers for all sinners.
Bring them back to your love through our example,
so that with them we may praise you
and celebrate our thanks through Christ our Lord.**

12. Hymn: If desired, a hymn may be sung.

Examination of Christian Living

13. Examination of conscience: See pages 99-141.

14. Silent prayer: For about five minutes, all remain in silence. Sitting or kneeling as they wish, they discuss their way of life with the Lord.

15. Community act of sorrow:

Reader or president:
**Lord, you have called us to be children of light.
Forgive us for choosing darkness and sin.
Lord, have mercy.**

All: *Lord, have mercy.*

**You have promised us your help in times of need.
Forgive us for neglecting your strength in our weakness.
Christ, have mercy.**

All: *Christ, have mercy.*

**You have come to give us eternal life.
Forgive us for refusing your gifts to us.
Lord, have mercy.**

All: *Lord, have mercy.*

16. Acclamation: A hymn may be sung.

Or a brief form of the general intercessions may be based on the theme, ending with the Lord's prayer (no. 17).

Conclusion of the Rite

17. Lord's prayer: This prayer is best sung by all. The president may prepare an introduction to this prayer, based on the theme of the service. For example:

**Let us pray to the Father of light
as Christ our Lord has taught us:**

Our Father . . .

18. Sacred action: The leader invites all to share the peace of Christ with one another, and introduces the rite in this way:

**Jesus gives his forgiveness and peace
to all the people of God.
Let us share his peace and love with one another.**

19. Invitation to the sacrament: The president may invite the congregation to celebrate the sacrament of penance after the bible service has ended.

20. Blessing: The leader may conclude with a simple blessing, or may use this form:

Let us bow before the Lord our God,
and ask him to bless us.

May God our Father bless us
for we are his children of light.

All: *Amen!*

May God the Son, Jesus Christ our Lord,
watch over and protect us.

All: *Amen!*

May God the Holy Spirit
lead us on the path of holiness.

All: *Amen!*

May our all-powerful God
— the Father, the + Son, and the Holy Spirit —
bless us and keep us for ever.

All: *Amen!*

21. Concluding hymn: All sing a seasonal hymn or song of praise.

JESUS FORGIVES US

Entrance Rite

1. Song

2. Enthroning the word of God

3. Greeting: After all make the sign of the cross, the president greets the assembled community with one of the following, adapted as necessary:

> 3 Jn. 15
> 1 Cor. 1: 3
> 2 Cor. 13: 11
> Col. 1: 2

4. Opening prayer: The president may choose a suitable prayer from the sacramentary; or one may be composed, based on the theme developed in the readings chosen for this celebration. One example of this prayer:

> **Let us pray to our Father in heaven.**
> **He sent Jesus to lead us away from sin**
> **and bring us into the kingdom of light:**

> All pause for silent prayer.

> **God of power and mercy,**
> **keep all hindrance to our progress far away,**
> **that our path may be free of all obstructions,**
> **both of body or mind,**
> **in the pursuit of your will.**

> **We ask this in the name**
> **of our Lord Jesus Christ, your Son,**
> **who lives and reigns with you and the Holy Spirit,**
> **one God, for ever and ever.**

Liturgy of the Word

God's word invites us to conversion and renewal of our life by proclaiming that Christ's death and rising have freed us from slavery to sin, and have made us his people of praise.

5. Reading from the word of God: The first reading may be chosen from:

Is. 55: 1-11	lectionary, no. 42
Jer. 7: 23-28	241
Ezek. 36: 23-28	42
2 Cor. 5: 17-21	33
1 Pet. 1: 17-23	47

6. Meditative silence: A few moments of silence follow the reading, allowing all to reflect and pray in response to the word they have heard in faith.

7. Psalm: After silent prayer, a psalm or hymn is sung.

8. Second reading: If a second reading is used, it may be chosen from one of the New Testament texts above, or from readings in the seasonal lectionary. A moment of silent prayer follows this reading.

A gospel acclamation may be chosen from CBW II.

9. Gospel reading:

Mk. 2: 1-12	lectionary, no. 81
Mk. 2: 15-17	310
Lk. 7: 36-50	94
Lk. 15: 1-13	—
Jn. 3: 16-21	269
Jn. 20: 19-23	773

10. Homily: The president proclaims the wonderful works and mercy of God as revealed in the scripture texts, and leads the assembly to prayer for sinners, to a reflective examination of conscience, and to repentance.

11. Prayer for sinners: The leader invites all to pray:

Let us pray for sinners
and ask God to forgive them:

All pause for silent prayer.

Heavenly Father,
you do not want sinners to die,
but to live in grace and serve you in love.
Look upon the people of the world
and draw them back to you through Christ.

With him we pray:
Father, forgive them, for they know not what they do!

Send your Spirit to soften hard hearts,
to bend rigid wills,
to warm those who are indifferent to you,
and to lead them to give you praise.

Father,
forgive us our sins
and listen to our prayers for all sinners.
Bring them back to your love through our example,
so that with them we may praise you
and celebrate our thanks through Christ our Lord.

12. Hymn: If desired, a hymn may be sung.

Examination of Christian Living

13. Examination of conscience: See pages 99-141.

14. Silent prayer: For about five minutes, all remain in silence. Sitting or kneeling as they wish, they discuss their way of life with the Lord.

15. Community act of sorrow:

Reader or president:
Lord, you first chose us as your friends in baptism:
forgive us for our weakness in living the life of grace.
Lord, have mercy.

All: *Lord, have mercy.*

Lord, you call us to follow you:
forgive us for failing to listen to you.
Christ, have mercy.

All: *Christ, have mercy.*

Lord, you ask us to serve those in need:
forgive us for not helping our brothers and sisters in need.
Lord, have mercy.

All: *Lord, have mercy.*

16. Acclamation: A hymn may be sung.

Or a brief form of the general intercessions may be based on the theme, ending with the Lord's prayer (no. 17).

Conclusion of the Rite

17. Lord's prayer: This prayer is best sung by all. The president may prepare an introduction to this prayer, based on the theme of the service. For example:

God has called us to be his people of praise.
Let us pray with Jesus to our Father:

Our Father . . .

18. Sacred action: The leader invites all to share the peace of Christ with one another, and introduces the rite in this way:

Jesus gives his forgiveness and peace
to all the people of God.
Let us share his peace and love with one another.

19. Invitation to the sacrament: The president may invite the congregation to celebrate the sacrament of penance after the bible service has ended.

20. Blessing: The leader may conclude with a simple blessing, or may use this form:

**May God our loving Father
bless you for ever.**

All: *Amen!*

**May God the Son, our Lord Jesus Christ,
bless you in all your actions.**

All: *Amen!*

**May God the Holy Spirit
bless you and be with you for ever.**

All: *Amen!*

**May you be protected and blessed,
and made strong in faith, hope, and love
by our all-powerful and loving God,
the Father, the + Son, and the Holy Spirit.**

All: *Amen!*

21. Concluding hymn: All sing a scasonal hymn or song of praise.

EXAMINATION OF CONSCIENCE

A form of examination of conscience is usually included in each penance celebration. The examination of conscience in many ways is the heart of any penance celebration. It is the time in which those who gather to celebrate the forgiving love of the Father review their lives in relationship to self, others, God and the world.

Purpose: The examination of conscience gives individuals within the parish community time to stop and reflect on their efforts to overcome sin and to live the life of grace. Having heard the word of God announced in the scripture readings, those gathered pause to take note of the radical demand of the Lord to give up all sin and to follow him in his death and resurrection to new life.

Focused upon the gospel demands of love and grace, the examination of conscience restores dignity to those who are sons and daughters of the loving Father. It calls individuals to an honest search for truth and sincerity in leading the Christian life. It remembers that in our baptism the journey with Christ is initiated and still continues.

A time for silence: To realize the benefits of this examination, inner silence is absolutely necessary. It is the silence encouraged by the psalmist when he asked for quiet before the Lord and patient waiting for his presence in the midst of distraction and anxiety (see Ps. 37: 7). The Lord calls us once more to conversion, and we hear his invitation when we are in silence and peace. Inner silence enables us to come face to face with the true situation in our Christian life.

Method: Normally, in a penance celebration, to assist in the examination of conscience, points for reflection are provided by the leader or reader(s). These are read in a slow meditative way; pauses for silent prayer and reflection are provided following each series of points presented.

The fifteen examinations of conscience presented in this book are examples of possible approaches that may be used in any penance celebration. They may be adapted for use in the local parish; they may provide a starting point for planning groups in their efforts to develop their own examinations.

The format for the examination of conscience may vary: some flow directly from the Lord's teaching in the scriptures; others look at the main responsibilities in the Christian life; still others consider how one relates to family, friends and the needy of the world.

Two readers may be used to present the various points for reflection to those who are examining their consciences.

The Rite of Penance, Canadian edition, Appendix III, pages 155-159, presents another model for the examination of conscience.

A

Leader:
Let us turn to God our Father and ask his mercy,
that we may turn away from our sins
and come back to him in love.

Reader:
Do I show reverence and respect for God and his name?
Do I thank him for calling me
to be a member of his people of praise?
Do I praise and thank God each day?
Do I love him with my whole heart and strength?

All pause for a moment of silent prayer and reflection.

Reader:
Do I keep the Lord's day holy by prayer and worship,
by reading God's word, and by taking adequate rest?
Do I take a full part in community worship?
Or do I profane the Lord's day by unbecoming activities and excesses?

All pause for a moment of silent prayer and reflection.

Reader:
As a parish community,
do we praise God in all our efforts?
Are we trying to make our worship as perfect as possible?
Do we do everything in the name of Jesus for the glory of God?

All pause for a moment of silent prayer and reflection.

Reader:
Do I accept God's will as taught in the bible?
Do I respect the authority of Christ and his Church?
Do I obey and respect those in authority over me?
Am I a cause of rebellion to those in my charge?

All pause for a moment of silent prayer and reflection.

Reader:
Do I respect God's gift of life
by showing kindness and love to young and old?
Do I work to save the lives of the unborn,
and to bring about respect and dignity for all God's children?
Do I take reasonable care of my own health
and that of my own family?

All pause for a moment of silent prayer and reflection.

Reader:
Do we respect our bodies as temples of the Holy Spirit?
Do we obey God's will for marriage and family life?
Do we strive to remain pure in every thought, word, and deed?
Do we stand up for Christ in the face of the world's lax standards?

All pause for a moment of silent prayer and reflection.

Reader:
Do we control our appetite for more possessions?
Are we using them in order to give greater glory to God
and to work for our salvation?
Do we respect other people's rights to their own property?
Do we avoid pollution and destruction of the world God gives us?

All pause for a moment of silent prayer and reflection.

Reader:
Am I honest and straightforward in all things?
Do I tell the truth at all times,
saying *yes* when I mean *yes*, and *no* when I mean *no*?
Do we encourage truthfulness and honesty by all in our family?

All pause for a moment of silent prayer and reflection.

Reader:
Do I show my love for God by loving and serving others?
Do I serve God in joy?
Do I seek to give him thanks and praise through Christ
in everything I do?

All pause for a moment of silent prayer and reflection.

The parish council or liturgy committee may wish to add other reflective questions at this point.

The examination of conscience may conclude in this way:

Are we living as followers of Jesus Christ?
Do we live as God's people, holy and blameless in his sight?
Do we ask the Holy Spirit for guidance and strength
to love others as Jesus has loved us?

All pause for a moment of silent prayer and reflection.

Leader:
People of God,
Christ is calling us to turn away from our sins.
Die to sin, and live with Jesus for God.
Let his Spirit lead you back to him,
forgiving you and filling you with his love.

100

B

Leader:
**Let us turn to God our Father and ask his mercy,
that we may turn away from our sins
and come back to him in love.**

Reader:
**Am I seeking to know God's will for me
by listening to his word frequently?
Do I try to find out what Christ teaches,
and base my life on his will?
Is Christ the king and ruler of my life?**

All pause for a moment of silent prayer and reflection.

Reader:
**Do I continue to die to sin and live for God each day?
Am I willing to do God's will
and to help his kingdom come among us?
Do I take up my cross daily, and follow Christ?**

All pause for a moment of silent prayer and reflection.

Reader:
**Do I let Christ's values rule my life?
Am I seeking the kingdom of God first?
Do my actions proclaim to all that I follow Christ?**

All pause for a moment of silent prayer and reflection.

Reader:
**Am I trying to obey God's will for me
by carrying out the duties of my state in life?
Do I accept daily crosses as coming from the Father's hand?
Do I say, "Not my will, but yours be done," to the Father?**

All pause for a moment of silent prayer and reflection.

Reader:
**Do I love God with my whole heart,
and with all my strength?
Do I ask God to help me love him more?
How often do I think of God and talk with him?**

All pause for a moment of silent prayer and reflection.

Reader:
**Do I show my love for the other members of my family?
Am I trying to be more patient and understanding with them?
Do I try to get along with others in peace?
How often do we pray together?**

All pause for a moment of silent prayer and reflection.

Reader:
Do I keep all the commandments as God's will for me?
Do I pray in time of temptation and stress?
Do I put enough trust in God's love for me?

All pause for a moment of silent prayer and reflection.

Reader:
Do I take my full part in Mass each Sunday?
Do I make a reasonable contribution each week to my parish?
Do I share myself by taking part in the work of the parish?

All pause for a moment of silent prayer and reflection.

Reader:
Am I closer to God or more distant
than I was at this time last year?
What am I doing about my spiritual condition?
What does God want me to do?

All pause for a moment of silent prayer and reflection.

The parish council or liturgy committee may wish to add other reflective questions at this point.

The examination of conscience may conclude in this way:

Are we living as followers of Jesus Christ?
Do we live as God's people, holy and blameless in his sight?
Do we ask the Holy Spirit for guidance and strength
to love others as Jesus has loved us?

All pause for a moment of silent prayer and reflection.

Leader:
People of God,
prepare a way for the Lord.
Make his paths straight in your lives,
and smooth out the rough roads in your hearts.
Let his Spirit lead you back to him,
forgiving you and filling you with his love.

C

Leader:
Let us turn to God our Father and ask his mercy,
that we may repent of our sins
and turn back to him in love.

Reader:
Jesus has called us to be the light of the world,
to shine like him through the darkness.
In my words and conversations,
do I reflect the light of Christ?
Does my talk lead people closer to Jesus?

All pause for a moment of silent prayer and reflection.

Reader:
Do I think about God and his plans for me?
Are the things of God far from my thoughts?
Do I want to make his kingdom come?

All pause for a moment of silent prayer and reflection.

Reader:
Does Christ find a welcome in our home?
Do we pray as a family? as individuals?
Do we listen to God's word together?

All pause for a moment of silent prayer and reflection.

Reader:
Do I love Christ?
Do I obey his commandment to love others?
Am I ready to serve others as he did?

All pause for a moment of silent prayer and reflection.

Reader:
Am I working to make my parish community
shine with the light of Christ?
Am I trying to make it a community of prayer?
Do I try to promote better worship and celebration?
Do I serve in one of the parish ministries?

All pause for a moment of silent prayer and reflection.

Reader:
Do I keep God's commandments
and encourage others to do the same?
Do I let others' laughter keep me from doing right?
Do I pray each day for help to obey God's will?

All pause for a moment of silent prayer and reflection.

Reader:
During the past year,
have I grown in God's love or service?
Is my life pleasing to Christ?
Are there areas where he wants me to improve
so that I can reflect his light more fully?

All pause for a moment of silent prayer and reflection.

The parish council or liturgy committee may wish to add other reflective questions at this point.

The examination of conscience may conclude in this way:

Are we living as followers of Jesus Christ?
Do we live as God's people, holy and blameless in his sight?
Do we ask the Holy Spirit for guidance and strength
to love others as Jesus has loved us?

All pause for a moment of silent prayer and reflection.

Leader:
People of God,
Christ is calling us to turn away from our sins.
Die to sin, and live with Jesus for God.
Let his Spirit lead you back to him,
forgiving you and filling you with his love.

D

Leader:
**Let us turn to God our Father and ask his mercy,
that we may turn away from our sins
and come back to him in love.**

Reader:
**Do I trust Jesus?
Do I accept him as my Lord and savior?
Do I listen to his word? How often?
Am I waiting in hope for his coming?**

All pause for a moment of silent prayer and reflection.

Reader:
**Do I believe that Jesus is coming to judge me?
Am I ready for his coming?
What things in my life are against his will?
Is Jesus pleased with the life and actions
of our parish community?**

All pause for a moment of silent prayer and reflection.

Reader:
**Do I try to see Jesus in other people,
especially those who are in need, or down and out?
Do I support honest agencies
that work for poor and helpless individuals and nations?
Do I try to use my talents and gifts
to help other people and my parish community?**

All pause for a moment of silent prayer and reflection.

Reader:
**Do I refuse to open my heart and my purse
to people who need my help and understanding?
Do I despise people who are less fortunate?
Do I look down on others
because of their race, nationality, sex, or life styles?**

**Am I making it harder for others
to live in a human and dignified way?
How much of this world's resources do I waste?
Do I gather too many goods for myself and my family?**

All pause for a moment of silent prayer and reflection.

Reader:
**Do I pray every day?
Do I want God's kingdom to come among us?
Am I taking time every day to listen to God's word?
Do I encourage my family and other people to pray?
Does our parish teach us how to grow in prayer?**

All pause for a moment of silent prayer and reflection.

Reader:
Do I take a full part in the worship of this community?
Am I preparing by prayer and service
for our Sunday celebration?
Do we prepare as a family?

Are there other ways in which we could help
to make our parish worship more pleasing to God?
Have I offered to use my talents in our community?
Do we pray for those who are ministers in worship?

All pause for a moment of silent prayer and reflection.

Reader:
Do I see the duties of my state in life
as God's will for me?
Am I trying to know what God wants,
and doing it each day?
Am I seeking to do my best for Christ?
Do I respect and love those who are closest to me?

All pause for a moment of silent prayer and reflection.

Reader:
Do I respect the gifts of creation that God gives us?
Am I trying to be responsible in using this world?
Do I work with others to make the world
a better place for all to live?
Am I involved in overcoming injustice
in this community and in the world?
Am I working for justice and peace for all?

All pause for a moment of silent prayer and reflection.

The parish council or liturgy committee may wish to add other reflective questions at this point.

The examination of conscience may conclude in this way:

Are we living as followers of Jesus Christ?
Do we live as the people of God, holy and blameless in his sight?
Do we ask the Holy Spirit for guidance and strength
to love others as Jesus has loved us?

All pause for a moment of silent prayer and reflection.

Leader:
People of God,
prepare a way for the Lord.
Make his paths straight in your lives,
and smooth out the rough roads in your hearts.
Let his Spirit lead you back to him,
forgiving you and filling you with his love.

E

Leader:
**Let us turn to God our Father
and ask his mercy,
that we may repent of our sins
and turn back to him in love.**

Reader I:
**Jesus has told us to love God
with our whole heart and soul,
and with all our strength:**

**As individuals,
do we praise God for his glory?
Do we thank him for his gifts to us?
Do we praise him for helping us to overcome sin?**

All pause for a moment of silent prayer.

Reader II:
**Do we pray to God each day?
Do we come to God each day through Christ?
Do we remember that the Spirit is living within us?**

All pause for a moment of silent prayer.

Reader I:
**Do we try to use God's name in the right way?
Are we trying to be good members of our parish?
Are we using our talents for others and for the Church?
Do we take part fully in our community worship?**

All pause for a moment of silent prayer.

Reader I:
**As a community,
are we trying to offer better worship to God?
Is our Sunday celebration as good as it should be?
Are we devoting enough time and effort to God's service?**

All pause for a moment of silent prayer.

Reader II:
**Jesus has told us to love our neighbor
as we love ourselves,
to love one another as he has loved us:**

**As individuals,
are we trying to live our family life
according to the gospel of Jesus?
Is prayer important in our home?
Are we concentrating on our own entertainment
more than on the needs of others?**

All pause for a moment of silent prayer.

Reader I:
**Are we respectful toward the law and institutions
of our civil community?
Do we reject or despise laws made for the good of all?**

All pause for a moment of silent prayer.

Reader II:
**Do we respect the gift of life
that God has given to us and to other people?
Do we stand up with the Church
to defend the right to life?**

All pause for a moment of silent prayer.

Reader I:
**Are we honest in our dealings
with God, ourselves, and others?
Do we bend, ignore, or distort the truth?
Do we look at all things in the light of Christ?**

All pause for a moment of silent prayer.

Reader II:
**Do we listen to Christ and his Church
in our marriage and family life?
Do we believe Christ or the world
when it comes to what is right or wrong?
Are we followers of the gospel of Jesus?**

All pause for a moment of silent prayer.

Reader I:
**Do we carry out our civil responsibilities
by obeying the law,
by voting with care,
by paying our taxes,
by supporting good causes,
by speaking out against abuses?**

All pause for a moment of silent prayer.

Reader II:
**As a parish,
do we seek to love others as Christ has loved us?
Are our parish funds used in the service of others?
Do we let petty matters interest us
more than they should?**

All pause for a moment of silent prayer.

Reader I:

**As a community of Christ's brothers and sisters,
do we consider bingo more important than bread for others?
Are card parties as important as proper housing?
Do we spend more time on rummage sales
than on the rights of our brothers and sisters?
What are our parish priorities —
fun and entertainment for ourselves,
or prayer and service for others?**

All pause for a moment of silent prayer.

Reader II:

**Have we more concern with preserving property
than with protecting and promoting life?
Are we letting Christ or the world
direct our thoughts, our values, our lives?**

All pause for a moment of silent prayer.

The parish council or liturgy committee may wish to add other reflective questions at this point.

The examination of conscience concludes in this way:

Reader I:

**Are we living as followers of Jesus Christ?
Do we live as the people of God,
holy and blameless in his sight?
Do we ask the Holy Spirit for guidance and strength
to love others as Jesus has loved us?**

All pause for a moment of silent prayer.

Leader:

**People of God,
Christ is calling us to turn away from our sins.
Die to sin,
and live with Jesus for God.
Let his Spirit lead you back to him,
forgiving you and filling you with his love.**

F

Leader:
**Let us turn to God our Father,
and ask his mercy,
that we may repent of our sins
and turn back to him in love.**

Reader I:
**Do we ever remember how much our Father loves us?
Do we praise him as our God?
Do we thank him for sending his Son to save us?**

All pause for a moment of silent prayer.

Reader II:
**Do we remember what Jesus has done to save us?
Do we thank him for saving us from the power of Satan?
Do we love him?
How do we show our love for him?**

All pause for a moment of silent prayer.

Reader I:
**Do we take part in Sunday Mass as well as we can?
Is there room for improvement in our parish worship?
Do we pray at home every day?
Are we encouraging our family to pray together often?**

All pause for a moment of silent prayer.

Reader II:
**Do we try to recognize Christ among us
whenever we gather together in his name?
Do we read his word and listen to him?
Are we seeking to know God's will for us?**

All pause for a moment of silent prayer.

Reader I:
**Are we making any efforts — as individuals and as a parish —
to help those who are oppressed in our community
by poverty, racial hatred, or by our indifference?
Do we love Jesus in people who are hated or ignored?**

All pause for a moment of silent prayer.

Reader II:
**Are we hearing Christ's plea for help
in the voice of those who are sick, or feeble,
or overcome by disaster and tragedy,
or enmeshed by hatred and warfare?**

All pause for a moment of silent prayer.

Reader I:
Are we going along with evil in the world,
or do we stand up for Christ and for the will of God?
Do we stand with Christ and his Church
against war, killing, and abortion?
against revenge, lying, and theft?
against hunger and injustice?
against the rape of our planet and its people?

All pause for a moment of silent prayer.

Reader II:
Is our daily way of living
a sign of Christ's life in the world,
a light shining in the darkness,
or are we just the same as everyone else?
Are our ideas formed by the gospel,
or mainly by our neighbors, our newspapers,
by magazines, by radio and TV?

All pause for a moment of silent prayer.

Reader I:
Are we working with Christ to save the world?
Do we pray for sinners?
Are we giving wholesome guidance and example to the young?
Do we do penance often, and carry our daily cross with Christ?

All pause for a moment of silent prayer.

The parish council or liturgy committee may wish to add other reflective questions at this point.

Reader II:
Are we living as followers of Jesus Christ?
Do we live as the people of God,
holy and blameless in his sight?
Do we ask the Holy Spirit for guidance and strength
to love others as Jesus has loved us?

All pause for a moment of silent prayer.

Leader:
People of God,
prepare a way for the Lord.
Make his paths straight in your lives,
and smooth out the rough roads in your hearts.
Let his Spirit lead you back to him,
forgiving you and filling you with his love.

G

Leader:
Let us turn to God our Father,
and ask his mercy,
that we may repent of our sins,
follow Christ more closely,
and turn back to God in love.

Reader:
As an individual,
do I let God guide my life by his commandments?
How many minutes a day
do I spend in reading the word of God?
How much time do I give to prayer each day?

All pause for silent prayer.

Reader:
Do I develop the talents and graces God gives me,
and use them for the good of other people?
Do I accept the world's standards of right and wrong?
Do I know Christ's standards of good and evil,
and stand up for his teaching?

All pause for silent prayer.

Reader:
Am I generous in seeking to help other people?
Do I try to understand them,
and look for their good points and virtues?
In what ways can I improve my attitudes and approach
toward my family, neighbors, friends?

All pause for silent prayer.

Reader:
How seriously do I work with Christ to die to sin?
Am I honestly trying to live with Christ for God?

All pause for silent prayer.

Reader:
Our parish is a believing community,
called by God to carry on the work of Christ:
do we seek to see Jesus present among us?
Are we listening to the Spirit he gives us as our guide?
As a [parish] [community],
do we work for God's interests or for our own?

All pause for silent prayer.

Reader:

**Have we taken any positive action
as a [parish] [community] this year
to show we are a family of faith, love and prayer?
Does our record show that our [parish] [community]
is self-centered, spending most of our efforts on ourselves?**

**What does Jesus think of our activities
during the past year?**

All pause for silent prayer.

Reader:

**In the area where we live,
is our [parish] [community] an example of faith and love?
a model of concern for the sick, the suffering, the friendless?
a source of light and courage
for those in darkness and despair?**

All pause for silent prayer.

Reader:

**Do we bring Christ's truth and love to community needs?
Are we concerned for peace and development,
for missions and vocations and peace?
Do we spend our energy, time and resources
for God, for others, or mainly for ourselves?**

All pause for silent prayer.

Reader:

**How seriously are we working with Christ to die to sin?
Are we honestly trying to live with Christ for God?**

All pause for silent prayer.

Leader:

**People of God,
put sin out of your lives.
Die to sin,
and with Christ, live for God.
Let his Spirit lead you and guide you,
so that you may truly be his holy people.**

H

Leader:
**Let us turn to God our Father,
and ask his mercy,
that we may repent of our sins
and turn back to him in love.**

Reader:
**You are to be the light of the world,
so that all may see the good lives you lead,
and be led to praise your Father in heaven.**

Pause for silent reflection.

Reader:
Father, forgive us

All:
Let us see, O Lord, your mercy.

Reader:
**You are to obey his law, the will of God,
and to teach others to obey in faith,
to do his will on earth and to enter the kingdom.**

Pause for silent reflection.

Reader:
Father, forgive us.

All:
Let us see, O Lord, your mercy.

Reader:
**You are to forgive those who offend you,
to work for peace among all,
to be friendly and not angry with others.**

Pause for silent reflection.

Reader:
Father, forgive us.

All:
Let us see, O Lord, your mercy.

Reader:
**You are called to be pure of heart:
not to lust after others
or to sin with them;
you are to give up whatever leads you to sin.**

Pause for silent reflection.

Reader:
Father, forgive us.

All:
Let us see, O Lord, your mercy

Reader:
**You are to love your enemies,
and do good to those who harm you,
and not seek to take revenge.
You are to forgive them as God has forgiven you.
You are to be as perfect as your heavenly Father is!**

Pause for silent reflection.

Reader:
Father, forgive us.

All:
Let us see, O Lord, your mercy.

Reader:
**You are to help those in need,
but without showing off or boasting,
so that only your Father in heaven
may see your good deeds.**

Pause for silent reflection.

Reader:
Father, forgive us.

All:
Let us see, O Lord, your mercy.

Reader:
**You are to pray
in simple words to your heavenly Father,
trusting him in faith to give you what you need.**

Pause for silent reflection.

Reader:
Father, forgive us.

All:
Let us see, O Lord, your mercy.

Reader:
**You are to fast and do penance,
to follow Christ and carry your daily cross,
and not to boast of what you do for him.**

Pause for silent reflection.

Reader:
Father, forgive us.

All:
Let us see, O Lord, your mercy.

Reader:
**You are to serve God and not money,
to store up treasures in heaven,
to share what you have with others.**

Pause for silent reflection.

Reader:
Father, forgive us.

All:
Let us see, O Lord, your mercy.

Reader:
**You are to follow the hard way to eternal life,
to base your lives firmly on the word of God,
to bear fruit for the Lord by doing his will.**

Pause for silent reflection.

Reader:
Father, forgive us.

All:
Let us see, O Lord, your mercy.

Leader:
**People of God,
prepare a way for the Lord.
Make his paths straight in your lives,
and smooth out the rough roads in your hearts.
Let his Spirit lead you back to him,
forgiving you and filling you with his love.**

I

Leader:
Let us turn to God, our merciful Father,
asking him to guide us
as we examine our lives in truth and honesty.

Reader:
Father,
you have showered your love upon us in Christ,
but we have failed to love you in return.

All pause for a moment of silent prayer.

Leader:
Father, forgive us.

All:
Forgive us our sins,
and deliver us from all evil.

Reader:
For our failure to pray,
for our neglect of your saving word,
for our laziness in your service,
and our fear of living as your people should.

All pause for a moment of silent prayer.

Leader:
Father, forgive us.

All:
Forgive us our sins,
and deliver us from all evil.

Reader:
For our lack of preparation for Mass,
for our careless and worldly attitudes toward the Lord's day,
for our sluggish hearing of your word.

All pause for a moment of silent prayer.

Leader:
Father, forgive us.

All:
Forgive us our sins,
and deliver us from all evil.

Reader:
For failing to love you with our whole heart and strength,
for putting so many things ahead of you,
for not seeking your kingdom first,
for our deliberate refusals to do your will.

117

All pause for a moment of silent prayer.

Leader:
Father, forgive us.

All:
Forgive us our sins,
and deliver us from all evil.

Reader:
For our lack of concern for others,
for neglecting the sick, the aged, the lonely,
for failing to help people in their time of need,
for our preoccupation with petty things.

All pause for a moment of silent prayer.

Leader:
Father, forgive us.

All:
Forgive us our sins,
and deliver us from all evil.

Reader:
For neglecting to exercise Christian responsibility
in our families and in our communities,
for failing to give Christian leadership,
for fearing to profess our faith in our daily tasks.

All pause for a moment of silent prayer.

Leader:
Father, forgive us.

All:
Forgive us our sins,
and deliver us from all evil.

Reader:
For feasting instead of fasting,
for begrudging the pittances we give in alms,
for putting our comforts ahead of the needs and lives of others,
for considering our pleasures more important than your kingdom.

All pause for a moment of silent prayer.

Leader:
Father, forgive us.

All:
Forgive us our sins,
and deliver us from all evil.

Reader:

**For our unwillingness to forgive others
as generously as you forgive us,
for holding grudges and spite,
for bickering, back-biting, and gossip,
for failing to pray for others.**

All pause for a moment of silent prayer.

Leader:

Father, forgive us.

All:

*Forgive us our sins,
and deliver us from all evil.*

Reader:

**For our neglect of parish and community life,
for our failures at home,
for all the obstacles we have placed in the path of unity,
for our sins and faults and evil habits.**

All pause for a moment of silent prayer.

Leader:

Father, forgive us.

All:

*Forgive us our sins,
and deliver us from evil.*

Leader:

**People of God,
Christ is calling you
to turn away from your sins,
to believe in him as your saving Lord,
to die with him to sin,
and to live with him for God.**

J

Leader:
**Let us turn to God our forgiving Father and ask
that we may come back to him in faith and love
and in turn experience his mercy and forgiveness.**

Reader:
**Father,
for the times we have failed to give you first place,
when we did not seek your kingdom first,
when we failed to pray and sing your praises;
for neglecting to read your word.**

All pause for a moment of silent prayer and reflection.

Leader:
Lord, forgive us.

All:
Have mercy on us, Lord, for we have sinned.

Reader:
**For our failure to show respect for your holy name,
for our misuse of our power of speech.**

All pause for a moment of silent prayer and reflection.

Leader:
Lord, forgive us.

All:
Have mercy on us, Lord, for we have sinned.

Reader:
**For our careless attitude toward Sunday,
the day of the Lord Jesus,
for our poor preparation and celebration of Sunday Mass.**

All pause for a moment of silent prayer and reflection.

Leader:
Lord, forgive us.

All:
Have mercy on us, Lord, for we have sinned.

Reader:
**For our slowness in recognizing your voice speaking to us
through our pope, bishops and pastors,
through our parents, teachers and leaders.**

All pause for a moment of silent prayer and reflection.

Leader:
Lord, forgive us.

All:
Have mercy on us, Lord, for we have sinned.

Reader:
For the ways we have made others' lives harder,
for our failure to work for justice and peace,
for our silence in the face of crimes against life.

All pause for a moment of silent prayer and reflection.

Leader:
Lord, forgive us.

All:
Have mercy on us, Lord, for we have sinned.

Reader:
For our sins against purity,
by which we defile the temples of your Spirit;
for accepting the world's standards instead of yours.

All pause for a moment of silent prayer and reflection.

Leader:
Lord, forgive us.

All:
Have mercy on us, Lord, for we have sinned.

Reader:
For making property and wealth more important than people,
and for piling up treasure here instead of heaven;
for our envy of other people's talents and property;
for our destructive pollution of the world you have given us.

All pause for a moment of silent prayer and reflection.

Leader:
Lord, forgive us.

All:
Have mercy on us, Lord, for we have sinned.

Reader:
For the times we have refused to love our neighbor
or to serve your Son in those in need;
for the times we have loved ourselves more than you.

All pause for a moment of silent prayer and reflection.

Leader:
Lord, forgive us.

All:
Have mercy on us, Lord, for we have sinned.

Leader:
The time has come;
God's kingdom is near,
it is in our midst.

Turn away from your sins
and believe the Good News of our salvation,
for Jesus has come to save his people!

K

Leader:
Let us turn to God our Father and ask his mercy
that we may die to sin
and live for God.

Peace with Self

Reader I:
Jesus says: "Seek first the kingdom of heaven,
and all these things will be given to you."
— What are my goals and ambitions?
 Do I seek God's glory or my own?
— Who or what has first place in my life?
— Do I understand that my attachment to sin
 is the only thing that keeps God's peace at a distance?

Reader II:
Jesus says: "Where your treasure is, your heart will be."
— Where is my treasure?
 Am I seeking power and wealth for myself?
 Am I storing up treasure in heaven?

Reader I:
Jesus says: "Lift up your heads,
your salvation is at hand."
— Do I trust God for help and salvation,
 or do I despair and give up?
— Do I thank the Lord for my vocation in life,
 or do I complain and grumble unhappily?
— Do I think about the wonderful gifts God has given me?
 Do I thank him joyfully for all his gifts?

All pause for a moment of silent prayer and reflection.

Leader:
Father, grant us freedom.

All:
Free us, Lord, from the guilt of our sins.

Peace with Others

Reader I:
God says: "One who loves is patient and kind."
— Do I accept the faults of others,
 or am I always trying to correct them and change them?
— Do I take out my problems and worries on others?
— Do I start each day by resolving
 to be more kind and cheerful toward others?

123

Reader II:
God says: "One who loves is not jealous, conceited or proud."
— Do I build myself up by tearing down others?
  Am I always looking for ways of belittling other people?
— Am I big enough to praise others for the good they do?

Reader I:
God tells us: "One who loves is not selfish or irritable."
— How often do I go out of my way or hold my tongue
  in order to keep peace in things that don't matter?
— Am I for ever seeking my own rights?
  Does my comfort come before the needs of others?

Reader II:
Jesus says: "Love others as I have loved you."
— Do I really care about other people?
— Do I show in action what I proclaim in my words?
— Do I realize that I am a liar
  when I say I love God
  and yet do not help others who are in need?

Reader I:
God teaches us: "Parents, love your children, and care for them.
Children, love and obey your parents."
— Am I kind to others outside my home,
  and miserable with the members of my family?
— How real is the greeting of peace
  I share with my family on Sunday?
  What am I doing to make it more sincere?

All pause for a moment of silent prayer and reflection.

Leader:
Father, grant us freedom.

All:
Free us, Lord, from the guilt of our sins.

Peace with God

Reader I:
The Father says: "Listen to me,
for I am your God, and you are my people."
— Do we remember that God is our loving Father?
  Do we pray to him daily,
  taking time and effort to praise him?
  Do we continue to ask for our needs,
  even when he seems slow to answer?
— Do we come together to celebrate Sunday Mass
  as an act of praise and thanksgiving?

124

Reader II:

Jesus assures us: "My grace is sufficient for you."
— Do I trick myself into thinking
    that I cannot or should not keep God's commands?
    Do I claim it is too hard to be pure,
    or foolish to be honest in business?
— Do I turn to Jesus in time of temptation?
— Am I striving to love God with my whole heart,
    with all my mind and all my strength?
— Do I pray for help to grow in God's love?

Reader I:

God reminds us: "Thin sowing means thin reaping."
— How generous are we with God?
    Do we take time to work for his glory?
    Do we work for the Church and for the missions?
— How important — or unimportant — is God
    in the life of our family?
— How much time did I spend last week
    on my own amusement and entertainment,
    and how little in God's interests?

All pause for a moment of silent prayer and reflection.

Leader:
Father, grant us freedom.

All:
Free us, Lord, from the guilt of our sins.

World Peace

Reader II:

**Jesus says: "I was hungry and thirsty
and you would not give me anything."**
— What efforts are we making
    at helping hungry nations become self-sufficient?
— Do we ever write our M.P. and other legislators
    on behalf of positive legislation
    for developing countries?

Reader I:

**Jesus says: "I was sick and in prison
and you would not come to visit me."**
— Do we make any effort to visit
    the sick and aged in our community?
    Do we ever try to bring joy into their lives?
— Do we work with those who are handicapped?
— Do we pray for the sick and the dying?

Reader II:

**Jesus says: "I needed clothing and shelter
and you would not give me help."**

**— Are we at all concerned about the needs
of people who are less well off?
What are we doing to promote social justice
in our community and country?**

**— How is our parish community showing concern
for people in dire poverty at home and abroad?**

All pause for a moment of silent prayer and reflection.

Leader:

Father, grant us freedom.

All:

Free us, Lord, from the guilt of our sins.

Leader:

**The time has come;
God's kingdom is near,
it is in our midst.**

**Turn away from your sins,
and believe the Good News of our salvation,
for Jesus has come to save his people!**

L

Leader:
**Let us turn to our loving Father and ask
that we may be forgiven our sins
and grow in the life of grace.**

Reader I:
**For our failure to carry our cross daily,
our unwillingness to share in your Son's suffering
and build up his body, your Church.**

Reader II:
**For our neglect of reading your word,
for our reluctance to listen to your Spirit.**

Reader I:
**For the days we have neglected prayer
because we were lazy, cold or indifferent.**

All pause for a moment of silent prayer and reflection.

Leader:
Father, be merciful unto us.

All:
Lord, grant us forgiveness.

Reader I:
**For missing or ignoring opportunities
of sharing our faith with friends and neighbors.**

Reader II:
**For the times we have been hardhearted,
refusing to forgive others,
and yet expecting you to forgive us.**

Reader I:
**For the times we have preferred
our own amusement or leisure
instead of doing your work.**

All pause for a moment of silent prayer and reflection.

Leader:
Father, be merciful unto us.

All:
Lord, grant us forgiveness.

Reader II:
**For the ways we have abused your creation
instead of singing its praises to you, Father.**

Reader I:
**For our lack of concern for peace in the world,
and for your Church's work and missions.**

Reader II:
**For the ease with which we turn our parish community
from working for your glory and the salvation of the world
to seeking fun and games and entertainment.**

All pause for a moment of silent prayer and reflection.

Leader:
Father, be merciful unto us.

All:
Lord, grant us forgiveness.

Reader I:
**For the times we have chosen sin
instead of doing your will.**

Reader II:
**For our sins against purity,
by which we defile the temples of your Spirit,
and for accepting the world's standards instead of yours.**

All pause for a moment of silent prayer and reflection.

Reader II:
**For our lack of generosity
toward you and all your people.**

Reader I:
**Father,
for the times we have been blind and insensitive
to the needs and sorrows of others.**

Reader II:
**For our failure to show real concern
for those who are starving, sick and homeless
because of natural disasters.**

All pause for a moment of silent prayer and reflection.

Leader:
Father, be merciful unto us.

All:
Lord, grant us forgiveness.

Leader:
**The time has come;
God's kingdom is near,
it is in our midst.
Turn away from your sins,
and believe the Good News of our salvation,
for Jesus has come to save his people!**

M

Leader:
The Lord speaks words of compassion and forgiveness to us.
Let us listen to his words,
to discover where we are failing to follow him.
Let us ask his help to be converted,
and to rebuild our lives in his service.

Faith or Fear

Leader:
The apostles were overcome by fear during a storm at sea.
When they cried out in fright,
"Save us, Lord!"
he answered: "Why are you frightened?
How little faith you have!"
Then he commanded the winds and waves,
and there was a great calm.

Reader I:
Do I have a deep faith in Jesus?
Do I trust in him, and rely on him alone to save me?
How often do I ask him to strengthen my faith?
Do I try to deepen it by prayerful reading of the gospels?

Reader II:
Do I try to see God's hand in events?
Do I realize that hardships and crosses
are his way of deepening our faith?
Do I remember that Jesus himself
learned to be obedient to God,
and for this reason
he is the source of salvation to all who believe in him?

Reader I:
Do I trust in God's loving care,
in his grace and strength,
or do I try to save myself
as though I did not need his help?

All pause for a moment of silent prayer and reflection.

Prayer

Leader:

By his example and his words, Jesus teaches us to pray.
He prays frequently,
even spending whole nights in prayer to his Father.
He prays before making important decisions.
He prays in suffering.
Jesus teaches us to ask God for what we need,
for our "Father in heaven will give good things
to those who ask for them."
He teaches us to persevere,
not to give up easily.
St. Paul reminds us:
"The Spirit comes to help us" to pray,
to help us put all our concerns before God.

Reader II:

Do I pray as Jesus teaches us?
How well do I pray? How often?
Do I pray in times of need?
Do I ever turn to God to praise him and thank him?

Reader I:

What kind of example of prayer life do I give
to those in my care?
Do I encourage and help them
to deepen their spirit of prayer?

Reader II:

Are we narrow or generous in our praying?
Do we pray for others: for our parish; for those in need;
for our spiritual and civil leaders;
for Christians in our community and around the world;
for peace and justice in the world?

Reader I:

Are we trying to grow in our prayer life?
in personal and family prayer?
in our parish [community] worship?

All pause for a moment of silent prayer and reflection.

Eager to Do God's Will

Leader:

Jesus encourages us to be eager to do God's will.
"My food," he tells us,
"is to obey the will of the Father who sent me."
In the garden, he accepts the suffering and death that God gives him.
"Not my will, Father, but your will be done."

130

He reminds us:
"The person who does what my Father wants him to do
is my brother, my sister."
Jesus invites us to give service from our hearts
and teaches us to pray:
"Father, may your will be done
on earth as in heaven."

Reader II:
What is my attitude toward God's will for me?
Do I give lip service or service from the heart?
Do I resent God's law as an interference in my life,
or do I see him as our loving Father,
showing us right from wrong,
helping us to grow in our love for him?

Reader I:
Do I base my life on the Lord's commandment
to love God with all my strength
and to love my neighbor as myself?

Reader II:
Do I look for ways of spreading God's love in the world?
Can people see Christ in my actions and words?
Does my life lead people to Christ or away from him?

All pause for a moment of silent prayer and reflection.

Forgiving Others

Leader:
While dying on the cross,
Jesus prays for his executioners and for all of us,
for our sins are the cause of his death:
"Father, forgive them,
for they do not know what they are doing."
Jesus teaches us to pray to God:
"Forgive us our sins
as we forgive those who sin against us."

Reader I:
Do I hold grudges against others
who have done me some real or imaginary harm?

Reader II:
Do I keep bringing up other people's past faults and failings?
Am I doing this to avoid looking at my own weaknesses?
Am I ready to forgive others
as generously as Jesus forgives me?

All pause for a moment of silent prayer and reflection.

Do This in My Memory

Leader:
**In baptism Jesus made us God's beloved people,
chosen in Christ from all eternity.
Filled with his Spirit and called to be holy,
we are a royal nation of priests,
chosen to sing God's praise.
At the last supper, Jesus tells us to remember him
by celebrating his supper together.**

Reader I:
**Modern society considers Sunday less as the Lord's day,
and more as a holiday.
Let us ask ourselves:
As God's people in this community,
how seriously do we take our responsibility to praise him
by taking a full and active part in the weekly celebration of Mass?**

Reader II:
**Do we see Sunday Mass as our response to God's invitation
to gather us together around his altar
to hear his word, praise his name, and eat the bread of life?
Do we come to remember the death and rising of the Lord Jesus?**

Reader I:
**What contribution do I make to our community celebration?
If already a reader, choir member, server or usher,
am I doing my best for God's glory?
How can our family help to make our parish celebration better?**

All pause for a moment of silent prayer and reflection.

End of Examination

Reader:
**Listen, people of God,
the Lord is speaking to us:**

Leader:
**"Now is the acceptable time,
today is the day of salvation."**

Reader:
**"The right time has come, and the kingdom of God is near!
Turn away from your sins
and believe the good news" of your salvation!**

Leader:
**"Harden not your hearts today,
but listen to the word of the Lord."**

N

Leader:

**God our Father has sent Jesus to save us,
to bring us from the kingdom of darkness
into his own kingdom of light.
Though we have been called
to be the children of light,
we have often chosen darkness and sin.
Guided by the Holy Spirit,
let us open our hearts to God's word,
admitting where we fail to follow Christ
and seeing how we need to improve.
Let us ask his help to be converted,
that we may once more live as the children of light,
as God wants his beloved people to live.**

Light of the World

Reader I:

**Jesus is the light of the world,
but in his wisdom, he sends us forth
to be the light of the world today.
We are called to do our good deeds before others
so that they will see the good we do
and give praise to the Father.**

Reader II:

**What sort of example of Christian living
do I give to my family?
Do I stand up for my faith
by my daily words and actions
at home, at work, at school, at play?**

Reader I:

**Does my whole manner of life —
my possessions, my recreation,
my language, my honesty —
lead people to Christ, or away from him?**

Reader II:

**Do I help my city [town, township] become better
by personal involvement in its affairs?
How much co-operation and leadership have I given
in the life and work of our parish community?**

All pause for a moment of silent prayer and reflection.

Leader:

Father, you sent your Son to be the light in the darkness.

All:

Open our hearts to your mercy and compassion.

Listening to the Lord

Leader:
**We do not live on bread alone,
but on every word spoken by God.
His words are a lamp to guide us,
a light for our path.**

**Lord Jesus,
you have the words of eternal life!
Open our eyes so that we may see
the wonderful truths in your law.**

Reader I:
**Do I read the word of God each day?
Is the bible the basis of my prayer?
Is God's word ever read aloud in our home?**

Reader II:
**Do we listen with faith to the readings at Mass?
During the week,
do we try to recall the Sunday gospel message?
Are we opening our heart to the Spirit
so that he may guide us in our daily living?**

Reader I:
**What sort of Christian reading matter is in our home?
Do we read religious books and papers
that will help us grow in our faith?
Are we trying to share our enthusiasm for Christ?**

All pause for a moment of silent prayer and reflection.

Leader:
Father, you sent your Son to be the light in the darkness.

All:
Open our hearts to your mercy and compassion.

Living As People of Light

Leader:
**Do not live according to the behavior of the world around you,
but let God change you inwardly
by a completely new way of thinking.**

**Jesus tells us:
Sell your belongings and give the money to the poor.
Store up your riches in heaven,
for your heart will always be
where your treasure is.**

Everyone will hate you because of me.
If the world hates you,
you must remember it has hated me first.
If you belonged to the world,
it would love you as its own.
But I have chosen you from this world,
and you do not belong to it.
If they persecuted me,
they will persecute you too.

Do not let evil defeat you;
instead, conquer evil with good.
I will not leave you alone;
I will come back to you.
I will ask the Father,
and he will give you another helper,
the Spirit of truth,
to stay with you for ever.

Reader II:
As an individual,
do I tend to follow the world's standards
instead of standing up for Christ's truth?
Is my personal treasure in heaven,
or is my heart kept at a distance from Jesus
by too much involvement in things?

Reader I:
As a parish community,
do we use our money and energy
for Jesus and his poor,
or for our own small goals?
What do we do for the helpless
at home and abroad?
How seriously do we support the missions?

Reader II:
Do we let the world lead us,
or are we giving Christian witness to others?
What did we do for Christ in the past year?

Reader I:
Are we ready to stand up for Christ at any cost?
Do we avoid persecution by being timid?
Do we talk and pray
in order to avoid action for justice
in the light of the gospel?

Reader II:
Are we discouraged by evil?
Do we turn daily to the Spirit
for light and guidance
to bring Christ's truth, joy and peace
into the lives and affairs of the world?

All pause for a moment of silent prayer and reflection.

Leader:
Father, you sent your Son to be the light in the darkness.

All:
Open our hearts to your mercy and compassion.

Prayer and Worship

Leader:
Jesus teaches us to pray in public
as well as in private,
for ourselves as well as for others.
We are to offer ourselves
as a living sacrifice to God,
dedicated to his service and pleasing to him.
Jesus invites us to be perfect,
as perfect as our heavenly Father is.

Reader I:
Do I seek God's light and strength
at the beginning of each day?
Do I end each day with praise and thanks,
with sorrow and good resolution,
with a prayer for help to do better tomorrow?

Reader II:
When I neglect to pray, do I realize
that I am failing to give glory to God?
Do I encourage prayer at home
among the members of our family?

Reader I:
Am I dedicated to serving Jesus Christ?
Am I trying to please him?
Do I seek to be perfect,
to make my life a living sacrifice of praise?
Am I doing every action for God's honor and glory?

All pause for a moment of silent prayer and reflection.

Leader:
Father, you sent your Son to be the light in the darkness.

All:
Open our hearts to your mercy and compassion.

Living Our Faith

Leader:
**Jesus promised the world
that it would recognize his followers
by their love for one another.
He sent us to show this love to others
so that we might lead them to the Father.**

Reader I:
**Do we live our daily lives
by Christ's standards or by the world's?
Do we do good actions in order to show off,
so that others will think we are holy?**

Reader II:
**Do we try to show love and kindness
to others by our daily actions?
How do we treat our relatives and neighbors?
How do we act toward strangers?**

All pause for a moment of silent prayer and reflection.

Leader:
Father, you sent your Son to be the light in the darkness.

All:
Open our hearts to your mercy and compassion.

Reader I:
**Jesus says to each of us:
without me, you can do nothing.
But in him, we can do all things.
He calls us to bear much fruit, eternal fruit.**

Reader II:
**He calls us to follow him, obedient to the Father,
loving and serving his brothers and sisters.**

Leader:
**The right time has come,
and God's kingdom is near,
Turn away from your sins,
believe the good news of our salvation.**

O

Leader:
**The forgiving love of the Lord is constant
and always present.
Let us renew our faith in the Lord
as we express our sorrow
and turn away from sin and live for God.**

Forgiving Others

Leader:
**Jesus says to us:
"If you forgive others the wrongs they have done you,
your Father in heaven will forgive you.
But if you do not forgive others,
then your Father in heaven will not forgive the wrongs
you have done."**

Reader I:
**Am I ready to forgive others as fully as Jesus forgives me?
Do I hold grudges against others
who have done me some real or imaginary harm?
Do I keep bringing up the past faults and failings of others,
and throw them in their faces?**

All pause for a moment of silent prayer and reflection.

Leader:
Father, open our hearts to your mercy.

All:
Lord, have mercy on your people.

Listening to the Word of God

Leader:
**Jesus tells us the parable of the sower and the seed:
"The sower sows God's message.
Some people hear the message, and receive it gladly.
But it doesn't sink deep into them,
and they don't last long.
But other people are like the seeds sown in good soil.
They hear the message, accept it, and bear fruit."**

Reader I:
**How do I listen to the word of God?
Am I eager to hear more about the teaching of Jesus?
Do I listen with attention while I hear his word read?
Do I open my heart so that God may send his Spirit
to stir me to greater, more loving service?**

Reader II:
How do I listen to the homily at Mass?
Do I make any effort to read the bible, which is God's own word?
Do I let God speak to me through nature,
through events in my daily life,
through the life of my parish?
When the Lord is speaking to me,
do I harden my heart,
or do I listen and respond to his invitation?

All pause for a moment of silent prayer and reflection.

Leader:
Father, open our hearts to your mercy.

All:
Lord, have mercy on your people.

Prayer

Leader:
By his example as well as by his words,
Jesus teaches us to pray:
"Ask, and you will receive;
seek, and you will find;
knock, and the door will be opened to you.
For all who ask will receive,
all who seek will find,
and the door will be opened to all who knock.
Your Father in heaven will give good things
to those who ask him."

Reader I:
Do I talk with God regularly? every day?
Or do I come running to God only when I'm in trouble?
Do I ever think of praising him or thanking him
for all he does for us?
Is praying a bore? a hard job?
Do I remember that Jesus has given me his Holy Spirit
to live in me and help me to pray?

Reader II:
As a parent, am I teaching my family by my daily example
to turn to God in prayer?
Is grace at meals neglected in our home?
Is it a meaningless ritual?
Or is it a time to thank God for all his gifts to us?
Am I selfish in my prayer,
or do I remember to pray for other people, for sinners,
for the Church in the modern world,
for people who are being persecuted for their faith?

All pause for a moment of silent prayer and reflection.

Leader:
Father, open our hearts to your mercy.

All:
Lord, have mercy on your people.

Carrying the Cross

Leader:
Jesus warns us:
"All who want to come with me,
must forget themselves,
take up their cross every day
and follow me."

Reader I:
Am I so busy being comfortable that I forget what Jesus teaches
about carrying his cross daily?
Do I look at suffering as a total evil,
or do I see God's hand in it?

Reader II:
Do I shrink from suffering, or grumble about it,
or do I try to accept my share in the suffering of Jesus?
Do I ever think of doing penance for the sins of the world,
to ask extra graces for those in special need of God's help?

All pause for a moment of silent prayer and reflection.

Leader:
Father, open our hearts to your mercy.

All:
Lord, have mercy on your people.

Light for All the Nations

Leader:
Jesus says to his followers:
"You are the light of the world.
Your light must shine before other people,
so that they will see the good things you do
and give praise to your Father in heaven."

Reader I:
Do I live as one reflecting the life of Jesus in the world?
What sort of example do I give at home, at work, at school,
in time of relaxation?

Reader II:
Do I give good example or scandal to others
in the way I speak, act and live?
Are other people brought closer to Jesus
or taken further away from him by the example I give?

All pause for a moment of silent prayer and reflection.

Leader:
Father, open our hearts to your mercy.

All:
Lord, have mercy on your people.

End of Examination

Reader I:
Listen, God is speaking to us:

Leader:
"Now is the acceptable time,
today is the day of salvation."

Reader II:
"The right time has come,
and the kingdom of God is near!
Turn away from your sins
and believe the good news" of your salvation!

Leader:
"Harden not your hearts today,
but listen to the word of the Lord."

Praise and Thanks — I

1. Loving Father,
   we thank you for bringing us to the beginning
   of a new season of reconciliation.
   During this time,
   you will bring many to experience your mercy and forgiveness.
   You will lead many to give you deeper praise,
   you will invite some to stand up as prophets to your people,
   and you will call some of us into eternal glory.

   Accept our praise and our suffering,
   our prayers and our efforts,
   our dying and our rising with your Son.
   Listen to our prayers for peace for all,
   and bless us as we bless your name.

   Send your Spirit to guide us in your ways,
   and lead us to you through Christ our Lord.   Amen!

2. Blessed are you, Lord God,
   ruler of all creation:
   you have made us your beloved children,
   brothers and sisters of Jesus our savior,
   and temples of your Spirit.

   Father, we thank you for making us Christians:
   give us your help to continue dying to sin
   and to live with Christ for you.
   Lead all people into your kingdom of light.

   All praise and glory be to you, Father,
   through your Son Jesus Christ,
   in the unity of your Holy Spirit,
   now and for ever.   Amen!

3. Blessed are you, Lord God, king of all creation:
   you have guided your people in prayer
   by the inspiration of your Holy Spirit.
   Accept the glory and honor we offer to you
   in union with the Church of all the ages
   through Jesus Christ our Lord.   Amen.

4. Blessed are you, O God,
   Lord of all the universe:
   you have chosen us as your children
   and have forgiven all our sins
   through the obedient death and glorious resurrection
   of your beloved Son, our Lord and savior.

   We praise you, Father of love,
   through Jesus your Son
   in the communion of your Holy Spirit,
   now and always and for ever.   Amen! Alleluia!

5. Blessed are you, Lord God:
   blessed are you for ever.
   Holy is your name:
   blessed are you for ever.
   Great is your mercy for your people:
   blessed are you for ever.   Amen!

6. All praise to you, Father in heaven,
   for leading us out of the darkness of sin
   into the light of your kingdom.
   We bless you for sending us your Son to save us,
   to die for us that we might die to sin,
   and to be raised that we might share your life.
   We thank you for giving us your Spirit of love
   to live in our hearts and lead us to you.

   All glory, praise, and honor be yours,
   Father, Son, and Holy Spirit,
   now and evermore.   Amen!

7. Blessed are you, Lord our God, king of all creation,
   and Father of your chosen people:
   we praise and thank you for your love.
   Help us to continue to praise you
   by our lives and by our worship.
   Send the Spirit of your Son into the hearts of all people,
   and lead them to eternal joy with you.

   Father, we ask this grace
   through Jesus Christ, our Lord and our brother,
   in the love of the Holy Spirit,
   now and for ever.   Amen!

8. Praise to you, Lord Jesus,
    image of the Father,
    our savior and our king:
    we rejoice in your forgiving love,
    and voice the praise of all creation for your Father.

    Send your Spirit to guide us at this time, we ask:
    with his light and grace,
    may he lead us and all your people
    along the ways of love and perfection.

    Help us to live holy and spotless lives, Lord Jesus,
    for we are called to give praise and glory to the Father
    through you, in the unity of the Holy Spirit:
    Praise to one God for ever and ever!   Amen!

9. Praise and glory are yours, Father of love,
    from all your beloved people
    in heaven and on earth.

    We praise you for your saving love,
    and thank you for giving us your Son as our Lord.
    Fill us with your Spirit of love,
    for we are your beloved children.

    Glory and honor are yours for evermore.   Amen!

10. All praise and glory are yours, Lord our God,
    king of the universe and Father of all:
    we thank you for choosing us to be your people,
    for adopting us as your children in Christ,
    and for sending your Spirit to lead us to you.

    Father, we bless you and give you glory
    through Christ our Lord and our brother
    in the love of your Holy Spirit,
    now and always and for ever.   Amen!

Praise and Thanks — II

1. God is our loving Father;
   we are his beloved children.
   All: *May his name be praised!*

   Our Father loves us so much
   that he has sent his only Son to be one of us.
   All: *All praise to God on high!*

   Our heavenly Father has given us his Holy Spirit
   to live within our hearts,
   to guide us in prayer,
   to make us his temples.
   All: *Glory to God in the highest!*

   In loving obedience,
   the Lord Jesus submitted to his Father's will,
   and stretched out his arms on the cross for us.
   All: *Praise and thanks to Jesus for ever!*

   In loving faithfulness, our Father raised Jesus to glory.
   All: *Blessed be God for ever and ever!*

   Our Father has called us in Christ to be his people of praise;
   he has forgiven us, and cleansed us from evil;
   he has made us his people of praise for ever.
   All: *Glory and praise are yours, Father,*
       through your Son Jesus Christ,
       in the love of your Holy Spirit,
       one God for ever and ever.   Amen!

2. God our Father, in his love for us, chose us in Christ to be his people. Before he
   made the world, he chose us to be holy, and to live faultless lives in his presence.
   He brought us out of Satan's kingdom of darkness, and into God's kingdom of
   light.
   All: *We praise God for his glorious grace,*
       for the gifts he has given us in his beloved Son!

   We are his chosen race, his royal priests, his own people, a holy nation. In his
   love, he decided to make us his sons and daughters through Jesus Christ.
   All: *We praise God for his glorious grace,*
       for the gifts he has given us in his beloved Son!

Our Father set us free by the death and rising of Christ, forgiving us our sins. He has told us about his great plan, which he wants to complete through his Son: he will bring all things together, with Christ as head.

All: *We praise God for his glorious grace,*
for the gifts he has given us in his beloved Son!

God chose us to be his beloved people in union with Christ, in order to accomplish his plan. He spoke the good news of salvation to us, and we believed.

All: *We praise God for his glorious grace,*
for the gifts he has given us in his beloved Son!

He has shown that we are his by giving us the Holy Spirit, as he promised us, his people. His Spirit brings love and freedom to all who belong to God.

All: *We praise God for his glorious grace,*
for the gifts he has given us in his beloved Son!

At one time we were not God's people, but now we are his people. Once we did not know his mercy, but now we have received his mercy.

All: *We praise God for his glorious grace,*
for the gifts he has given us in his beloved Son!

(Based on Eph. 1: 3-14; Rom. 5: 5; 1 Pet. 2: 9-10.)

3. **Lord Jesus Christ,**
   for calling us to follow you,
   for being our Lord and brother,
   for letting us share your cross,
   All: *We give you thanks, O Lord.*

   For sharing the life of the Father with us,
   for leading us in your light,
   for sending your Spirit to live in us,
   All: *We give you thanks, O Lord.*

   For baptizing us into your death,
   for raising us to new life with you,
   for calling us to be members of your kingdom,
   All: *We give you thanks, O Lord.*

   For marking us with your seal of life,
   for giving us faith and hope,
   for filling us with your love,
   All: *We give you thanks, O Lord.*

   For calling us to give you praise,
   for bringing us to eternal life,
   for letting us be your saints,
   All: *We give you thanks, O Lord.*

4. **Blessed are you, Lord God:**
   Blessed are you for ever.
   Holy is your name:
   All: *Blessed are you for ever.*

   You have sent your Son to be one of us:
   Blessed are you for ever.
   You love your people with deepest love:
   All: *Blessed are you for ever.*

   You have sent your Son to save us from sin:
   Blessed are you for ever.
   Great is your mercy for your people:
   All: *Blessed are you for ever.*

   You fill your children with joy:
   Blessed are you for ever.
   You call us to praise your name:
   All: *Blessed are you for ever.*

   Look with love on your holy Church:
   Blessed are you for ever.
   Send the Spirit of your Son into our hearts:
   All: *Blessed are you for ever.*

   Let us bring glory and praise to your name:
   Through Jesus Christ your Son:
   And in the love of your Holy Spirit:
   All: *Blessed are you for ever. Amen!*

5. This may be used as a personal prayer of praise. If said by a group, it may be
read in unison, or with alternating stanzas; or a reader may read the first few lines,
and have the group repeat the closing line of each stanza as a refrain.

   Blessed be God, for he has made us,
   and made this world for our use.
   All: *All praise to God for ever!*

   Blessed be our Father for his love,
   for he sent his only Son to save us.
   All: *All praise to God for ever!*

   Blessed be the Son of God,
   who came as one of us, and lived among us.
   All: *All praise to God for ever!*

   Blessed be the Holy Spirit,
   who leads us in the ways of God.
   All: *All praise to God for ever!*

Blessed be God, three persons in one:
to God be all honor and glory.
All: *All praise to God for ever!*

Other stanzas may be developed, in accord with the season or feast being celebrated. The final stanza should be a doxology, such as this:

All praise to God our Father
be given through the Son
in the unity of the Spirit,
one God for ever more.
All: *All praise to God for ever!*

6. **You bless us with the gift of life:**
    All: *Father, we give you thanks.*

    You give us your Son as our savior:
    All: *Father, we give you thanks.*

    You teach us the words of life:
    All: *Father, we give you thanks.*

    You cleanse us from our sins:
    All: *Father, we give you thanks.*

    You invite us to love you by loving others:
    All: *Father, we give you thanks.*

    You help us do good works for you:
    All: *Father, we give you thanks.*

    You grace us with talents to use for your glory:
    All: *Father, we give you thanks.*

    You nourish us with the bread of life:
    All: *Father, we give you thanks.*

    You give us the cup of salvation:
    All: *Father, we give you thanks.*

    You have gifted us with your Spirit:
    All: *Father, we give you thanks.*

    You promise us the joys of heaven:
    All: *Father, we give you thanks.*

    You call us to sing your praises forever:
    All: *Father, we give you thanks.*

    Beloved Father,
    you have given us all grace and life
    through the hands of Christ our savior.
    With Jesus, we bless your name.
    With him we thank you.
    With Christ our Lord, we pray to you:
    Our Father . . .

148

Prayers to the Trinity

A PRAYER TO THE TRINITY

Father, Son, and Holy Spirit,
we praise you and give you glory:
we bless you for calling us to be your holy people.

Remain in our hearts,
and guide us in our love and service.
Help us to let our light shine before others
and lead them to the way of faith.

Holy Trinity of love,
we praise you now and for ever. Amen!

PRAYER FOR GOD'S BLESSINGS

Blessed are you, Lord our God,
king of all ages:
from eternity you have called us to be your people,
to sing your praises at all times.

Bless us in our work and our prayer,
and grant that our lives may give you glory
through our words, our witness, and our worship.

We give you praise, Father,
through Jesus Christ, our brother and our Lord,
in the communion of your Holy Spirit,
one God for ever and ever. Amen!

FOR FIDELITY TO THE COVENANT

Blessed are you, Lord our God,
creator of the universe and Father of your people:
of old you chose Abraham to be our father in faith.
You made a covenant with your beloved people Israel,
and led them through the waters to your promised land.

We praise you, Father,
for making a new covenant with us in Jesus your Son.
Keep us in your love,
and let us always serve you faithfully.

All glory and praise are yours, Father,
through Jesus Christ our Lord,
in the love of the Holy Spirit,
now and always and for ever. Amen!

FOR THE MIND OF CHRIST

Ever-living God,
help us to think in the same way
that Jesus Christ thought.
From the abasement of his cross he stooped to death:
may we humble ourselves,
believing, obeying, living and dying for your glory.
May we be raised with Christ
into everlasting peace.

Father of love,
we ask this grace
in the name of the Lord Jesus.   Amen!

FOR HELP TO LIVE THE PASCHAL MYSTERY

Lord God, eternal Father,
you sent your Son to redeem the world
by his obedience to the point of death.

As your beloved people,
we ask you to grant our prayer:
teach us to crucify our flesh and its affections,
that we might die to sin and live for you.

May we die to sin with Christ,
rest with him,
and rise again with him to new life.
May we live with our Lord for ever.

Father, through Christ, our brother and our Lord,
we offer all glory and honor
to you, in the unity of the Holy Spirit:
Father, listen to our song of praise.
Alleluia!   Amen! Amen!

SEND YOUR SPIRIT — I

Lord Jesus,
send your Spirit into our hearts
so that we may die to sin
and live with you for the Father's glory,
now and always and for ever.   Amen!

SEND YOUR SPIRIT — II

Let us ask God our Father to send us his Spirit,
so that we may repent of our sins
and turn back to the way of God's peace.

All pause for a moment of silent prayer.

Father of mercy,
look upon us in love:
we are your Church, your beloved people.
Send your Holy Spirit into our hearts.
Help us to be truly sorry for our sins and failings,
for our treachery and ingratitude and hardness of heart.
Convert us, bring us back to you.
Teach us to live each day
in your love and service.

Father,
we ask this grace
in the name of Jesus our Lord.

SEND YOUR SPIRIT — III

Blessed are you, Lord God,
king of the universe:
you have forgiven us our sins
and have called us to be your holy people.
Give us your Spirit to guide us each day,
so that we may continue to die to sin
and to live with Jesus for you.

Father, we ask this grace
through Jesus, our brother and our Lord,
in the community of your Holy Spirit.   Amen!

151

Prayers for God's Gifts

FOR FAITH

Lord Jesus,
we praise you for saving us
by your dying and rising.
We give you glory for being the light of the world,
and for calling us to be your Church.

Deepen our faith and love.
Help us to obey the Father's will
and to spread his kingdom on earth.
Bring our praise and petitions to our Father,
for you are his beloved Son,
in the love of the Holy Spirit,
one God for ever. Amen!

FOR FORGIVENESS — I

All praise to you, Lord God,
Father of all creation:
you have loved us so deeply
that you gave your only Son, our savior,
to give us faith and eternal life.

Father,
we confess that we are sinners:
forgive us, and make us clean.
Listen to the pleading of your Son,
and forgive our sins and the sins of all humanity.
Help us to obey your commands
so that we may live in you,
and love and forgive others
as you have loved and forgiven us.

Father of love,
we bless your name
through Christ your Son
in the communion and love of your Spirit,
now and for evermore. Amen!

FOR FORGIVENESS — II

All praise and glory are yours,
Father of heaven and earth, Lord of all ages.
We praise you for the gifts you have given us,
and for the ways we have been led to use them
for your people and for your world.

Forgive us, Father, for our failures,
for neglecting your word,
for failing to listen to your Spirit,
for refusing to love you in others.

Let your Son be our leader and your Spirit our guide,
your word a lamp for our feet and strength for our hearts.
Help us to work for your honor and glory
and for the salvation of all your people.

Praise and honor and glory are yours, Father,
through your Son, our Lord and brother,
in the love and unity of your Holy Spirit
now and evermore. Amen!

FOR FORGIVENESS — III

Father,
lead us to return to your love.
Our king, bring us near to your service,
and cause us to return to your presence
in complete repentance.

Forgive us, Father, for we have sinned.
Pardon us, our king, for we have disobeyed,
and you pardon and forgive.
Blessed are you, O Lord:
you are gracious and grant abundant forgiveness. Amen!

FOR FORGIVENESS — IV

Let us pray to God our Father,
asking him to reconcile us with all,
for Jesus died that everyone might be saved:

All pause for silent prayer.

Praise to you, Lord God, king of the universe:
you have chosen us to be your beloved children,
united to you in your Son, our savior.

Lead us from sin
and help us to love and forgive others
as you have loved and forgiven us.

Father, we praise you and bless your name
through Jesus Christ our Lord.

FOR GUIDANCE

Blessed are you, God our Father, ruler of the universe:
you have called us as your people of praise,
and you have given us your Spirit to guide our prayer.
Teach us to give you glory
by singing the psalms in your honor
and by living each day in your love.

Blessed are you, God our Father,
now and for evermore. Amen!

FOR GOD'S HELP

Let us ask God for the strength we need
to live as his holy people.

All pause for silent prayer.

God our Father,
you have called us to be your beloved people;
you have rescued us from the kingdom of darkness and sin,
you have brought us into the kingdom of light.
Help us to continue to die to sin,
so that we may always live for you.

Father, we ask this through Jesus our Lord. Amen!

FOR JOY

Blessed are you, Lord God,
maker of heaven and earth:
you have given us your Spirit with his gifts.

Fill us with joy at your love for us,
and help us to love you by loving others
and by enjoying life in your service.

Glory to you, Father,
through your beloved Son,
in your Spirit of joy,
for ever and ever. Amen!

FOR LIGHT

Lord Jesus,
open our hearts and minds to the guidance of your Spirit.
Help us discern the Father's will for your Church today.
Do not let our weaknesses or prejudices hinder your work,
and teach us to do all we can
to make the kingdom of the Father come on earth.
Bring us to the harmony and unity given by your Spirit,
and make us one in praising God with you.

Hear us, Lord, for we are your beloved people. Amen!

FOR MERCY

Blessed are you, Lord God, king of all creation:
you have made this time and given it to us
so that we might live in your service.
Father, we thank you for your loving care.

Look with love and mercy on your Church around the world.
Help your people to be a forgiving community,
walking in the footsteps of Jesus our brother,
filled with love for you and for one another.
Let our faith and action bring you glory today,
and lead other people closer to you.

All praise and glory are yours, Father,
through Jesus your servant and your Son,
in the communion and love of your Spirit,
now and always and for ever more.   Amen!

FOR PEACE

Lord Jesus, we praise you:
bring peace into the world
by bringing peace into the hearts of all.
Help us to turn away from sin,
and to follow you in love and service.

Glory be yours, and honor
for ever and ever.

FOR SILENCE

Father,
teach us to be silent:
to listen to your Spirit,
to hear your voice and heed it,
to have time to reflect.

Father,
we ask this grace through Christ our Lord.   Amen!

FOR SINCERITY

All praise and glory are yours, Lord Jesus,
our brother and our Lord:
you have called us to be God's children,
and free us from sin and death.

Cleanse our hearts and minds, and purify our lips,
so that we may join you
in singing the praises of our heavenly Father.
Fill us with your Spirit,
and teach us to pray always.

All glory is yours, Lord Jesus,
for ever and ever. Amen!

FOR STRENGTH — I

Blessed are you, Lord God, Father of all:
you have made us your beloved children,
and call us to be your holy Church.

Remember the promises you have made to us,
and give us your strength and love as we follow Jesus your Son.
Fill us with the power of your Spirit,
lead many people to you by our prayer
and help us to live as children of light.

We give you praise, Father, through Christ your Son,
in the love and unity of your Holy Spirit,
for ever and ever. Amen!

FOR STRENGTH — II

All praise and glory are yours, loving Father,
maker and ruler of the universe:
we praise you for calling us to be your people,
your beloved sons and daughters.
Guide our community as we try to follow Jesus.
Fill us with love for those in need of our help,
and open our hearts to all.
Let your Spirit teach us to serve in love
and to praise you by our work and worship.

Father of all,
we praise you through Jesus Christ, our brother,
in the love of your Holy Spirit,
now and for ever. Amen!

FOR STRENGTH — III

Blessed are you, Lord God,
king of heaven and earth:
in love you have given us Jesus
to save us from sin and Satan
and to lead us back to you.

Strengthen us in our weakness
with the power of your Spirit,
and help us to follow your Son in love.

Father,
we give you praise
through Christ our Lord.   Amen!

Prayers for Ministers

FOR THE CHURCH — I

Blessed are you, Lord God,
ruler of all nations:
you have called us to be your Church,
your holy people of light and prayer.
You have set us aside to sing your praises.

All glory and honor is yours, heavenly Father,
through Jesus Christ, our Lord and brother,
in the love of your Holy Spirit,
always and for ever. Amen!

FOR THE CHURCH — II

Lord Jesus, we praise you.
Give us hearts of warm flesh, and not of cold stone.
Make us living stones in your eternal temple of praise.

Help us to be your Church,
and let our church reflect your love for us,
and our love for you.

Lord Jesus, we praise you. Amen!

FOR THE CHURCH — III

Lord Jesus Christ, our brother and our savior,
we praise you for your glory.
We thank you for calling us to be your Church,
and for sending us your Spirit
to guide us in our prayer and worship to the Father.

Look on us with love as we gather here to praise you.
Teach us to recognize your presence among us,
and help us to work, suffer, and pray with you.
Let our church be a sign of our faith and devotion,
a declaration of our willingness to serve you in others.

We praise you, Lord Jesus, and ask you to bless us,
for we are your beloved people,
one in the Holy Spirit, now and for ever. Amen!

158

AT THE BEGINNING OF PRAYER

Lord Jesus, Son of the Father,
we praise you and give you glory.

Teach us to pray in faith,
with hope and love,
with perseverance and with joy.
Give us your Spirit to help us to pray.
Guide our hearts and open our lips
to words of praise and petition for all in need.
Bring our prayers to our heavenly Father.

Lord Jesus,
we praise you now and for ever. Amen!

BEFORE MEDITATING ON THE SCRIPTURES

Lord Jesus,
we give you praise.
Speak to us as we read your word,
and send your Spirit into our hearts.
Guide us today and each day in your service,
for you are our way, our truth, our life.

Lord Jesus, we love you:
keep us in your love for ever and ever. Amen!

BEFORE PREPARING A PENANCE CELEBRATION

All praise and glory are yours, Father,
and we glorify your name.

Help us to prepare this penance celebration,
so that your people may praise you
and be filled with your word and the gift of forgiveness.
Let our celebration bring you glory
and lead us all to salvation and eternal life.

We ask this grace through Christ our Lord. Amen!

BEFORE THE MEETING OF THE PLANNING COMMITTEE

Blessed are you, Lord God,
king and ruler of all creation:
all glory, honor, and praise be yours.

Bless us as we gather here to promote your worship.
Cleanse our hearts from all evil,
and deepen your love in ourselves and in our families.

Throughout this meeting, guide us by your Spirit,
so that all we do and decide
will lead to your glory
and to the salvation of your people.

All praise is yours, Father,
through Christ our Lord. Amen!

PRAYER WHILE PREPARING A PENANCE CELEBRATION

All glory and praise are yours, Lord Jesus,
our brother and our savior:
by your obedient death you have given us life,
and by your rising,
you open heaven for all your people.

Fill us with your Holy Spirit,
and forgive us our sins.
Give us light to see the needs of our community,
courage to speak your word boldly,
and strength to continue serving all in love.

Help us to lead your people closer to your Father,
and bless us as we prepare this celebration.

Lord Jesus,
we give you glory and praise
today and for ever. Amen!

FOR THE PLANNING COMMITTEE

Blessed are you, heavenly Father, ruler of the universe:
you have chosen us as your people of praise,
and now we give you our thanks.

Pour your Spirit of love into our hearts.
Help us to work with your people
so that we may always praise your name.
Accept our worship through Jesus our Lord,
and be pleased with our efforts to serve you in others.

We offer our prayer to you, Father,
through Jesus Christ, our brother and our Lord,
in the love and unity of your Spirit,
now and for ever. Amen!

FOR LEADERS

Eternal Father,
look with love upon your people.
Guide the leaders you have chosen to lead us in prayer,
and give them the grace and guidance of your Spirit
so that they may bring us to you
in the footsteps of Jesus our Lord.

Father of glory,
we praise you and give you thanks
through Christ our savior
in the love and unity of your Spirit,
now and for ever. Amen!

A PREACHER'S PRAYER

Blessed are you, Lord God,
king of the universe:
you have sent your Word to become one of us,
Jesus Christ, our brother and savior.

Through his words you give us new life,
through his example you teach us love,
through his death and rising
you give us eternal life.

Father, send your Spirit into my heart
to guide me as I prepare to preach,
and to help me to speak your word to your people.
Open their hearts to hear your word,
and let me lead them to you
through Christ our Lord. Amen!

FOR MUSICIANS

All praise and glory are yours, heavenly Father:
you have called us to be your holy people,
and have set us aside to sing your praise.

Teach us to use our talents and voices for your glory
and for strengthening the faith of your Church.
Help us to persevere in practice and prayer,
so that we may show your love and mercy to others
and lead them closer to you.
Fill us with your Spirit of praise and love,
and let us live always for you.

All praise and thanks are yours, Father,
through Jesus our brother and our Lord. Amen!

FOR READERS — I

Praise to you, Lord God,
king of the universe,
and all glory to your name.
I praise you and thank you for calling me
to proclaim your word to your beloved people.

Open the hearts of all who worship with us,
so that they may hear your voice when I read.
Let nothing in my life or manner disturb your people
or close their hearts to the action of your Spirit.

Cleanse my heart and mind,
and open my lips so that I may proclaim your glory.

All praise to you, heavenly Father,
through the Lord Jesus
in the Holy Spirit,
now and for ever. Amen!

FOR READERS — II

Heavenly Father,
send the Spirit of your Son
into the hearts of your people.

Bless those who read the word in public,
and bless those who hear it.
Lead us to eternal light
by the paths of the Lord Jesus.

All glory and praise are yours, Father,
now and always and for ever. Amen!

OTHER PRAYERS

MARIAN ANTHEM

Blessed are you, mother of my Lord,
for you have believed the word of God.
In faith and love,
you have pondered the words and actions of God
in your life and the life of his people.

With Jesus we call you mother.
Pray for us,
and ask your Son to lead us to the Father.   Amen!

MARY: OUR MODEL IN PRAYER

All praise and glory are yours, almighty Father:
you have given us your Son to save us from sin.
We praise you for choosing Mary to be his mother,
for teaching her to believe your message,
for helping her to accept your holy will.

Strengthen us by your Spirit to be like Mary:
to ponder your word in our hearts,
to obey your will,
to love your Son,
to sing your praises each day.

Father,
we praise you through Jesus Christ your Son
in the love of your Spirit,
for ever and ever.   Amen!

FOR FAMILIES — I

Blessed are you, loving Father,
ruler of the universe:

You have given us your Son as our leader,
and have made us temples of your Holy Spirit.

Fill our family with your light and peace.
Have mercy on all who suffer,
and bring us to everlasting joy with you.

Father,
we bless your name for ever and ever.   Amen!

163

FOR FAMILIES — II

Heavenly Father,
we bless you and give you thanks
for your love and kindness.

Look on us with love
as we come together in Jesus' name.
Bless us all: mother and father,
Katie and Gregory, Andrew and Pauline.
Help us to love you, teach us to be good,
and help us to help other people.

Father, we pray to you through Jesus our Lord.   Amen!

PARENTS' PRAYER

All praise to you, Lord Jesus, lover of children:
bless our family,
and help us to lead our children to you.

Give us light and strength,
and courage when our task is difficult.
Let your Spirit fill us with love and peace,
so that we may help our children to love you.

All glory and praise are yours, Lord Jesus,
for ever and ever.   Amen!

FOR PARENTS

All members of the parish may wish to pray for the parents in the community of
faith:

Heavenly Father, giver of all good gifts,
look with love and mercy
on the parents in our parish.

Bless their lives,
and help them to reflect Christ's love for us.
Fill them with your love,
and let them bring your light into our community.

Help them to bring good children into this world.
Guide them as they raise their families.
Bless their children as they grow in wisdom, age, and grace.

Loving Father,
give your Spirit to each family in our parish,
and help us to follow your Son.

Father, we give you praise and glory
as we ask this grace through Christ our Lord
in the love of your Spirit,
now and for ever.   Amen!

APPENDIX

General confession and absolution

"Particular, occasional circumstances may render it lawful and even necessary to give general absolution to a number of penitents without their previous individual confession" (*Rite of Penance*, no. 31). Such a celebration takes place within a liturgy of the word. After the homily and examination of conscience, the rite is celebrated in the following order:

- Special instruction
- General expression of sorrow
- Litany or song
- Lord's prayer
- General absolution
- Proclamation of praise
- Blessing and dismissal.

The present name for this rite is "reconciliation of several penitents with general confession and absolution." An outline of the rite is given on pages 166-167. The ritual presents this rite in a rather truncated form, noting that it follows the format of the second rite (reconciliation of several penitents with individual confession and absolution), but with several exceptions given in nos. 35 and 60. These changes are indicated in the outline by an arrow, and are described below:

- *Instruction and penance* (rite, nos. 33, 35a, 60): The priest is to instruct the people to be disposed properly (see also Liturgy constitution, nos. 9, 11, 14, 19): this involves sorrow for our sins, and the resolution to turn away from them, to make up for scandal and harm, and to make an individual confession at a later time (described below).

Some act of satisfaction or penance is suggested for everyone. The penitent may also choose to add something further to this penance: such generosity is to be encouraged in response to God's forgiving love. It is to be noted that this is the only case in which a universal penance is given, and for one reason only — there is no way of giving individually tailored penances; in all other cases, a personal penance is given by the priest.

• *Sign of desiring absolution* (nos. 35b, 61): A public indication of wanting to be reconciled with the Church is made by all. This can be done by kneeling or by bowing the head, or by another sign appropriate in a particular culture. This public act is continued by a general admission of sin, such as *I confess to almighty God* from the order of Mass.

• *General absolution* (nos. 35c, 62): The priest extends his hands over the penitents (a form of imposition of hands), and says the prayer of absolution. He may use the regular form (as in no. 46), or the longer three-part formula, similar in style to the solemn blessings.

• *Obligation to individual confession* (nos. 34, 35a, 60): During the instruction, the priest points out the obligation of confessing each serious sin now being forgiven. This should be done before receiving general absolution again (unless "a just reason" prevents them), and certainly within the space of a year (unless this is seen as "morally impossible"). The two *unless* clauses are added in no. 34.

Rite

The reconciliation of several penitents with general confession and absolution is outlined in this table, which is based on the *Rite of Penance,* Introduction and Chapter III.

	Introduction No.	Rite No.
1. Before	15, 31-32	—
2. Introductory rites		
• Song	23	48
• Greeting	23	49
• Importance and meaning	23	49
• Opening prayer	23	50
3. Celebration of the word of God		
• Readings	24	51
— separated by psalm, hymn, silence		
— if only one reading: from gospel		
• Homily	25	52
→ • Instruction + penance	33, 35a	60
• Examination of conscience	26	53
4. Rite of reconciliation		
→ • Sign of desiring absolution	35b	61
• General confession	35b, 27	54
• Litany or song	35b, 27	61, 54
• Lord's prayer	35b, 27	61, 54
• Concluding prayer	—	54
→ • General absolution	35c	62
• Proclamation of praise	35d, 29	63
— invite to offer thanks		63, 56
— encourage to good works		56
— hymn		63, 56